James MacGillivray

2000

"YOU HAVE BEEN ALLOCATED UGANDA"

LETTERS FROM A DISTRICT OFFICER

ALAN FORWARD

ppc
POYNTINGTON PUBLISHING COMPANY
DORSET

Published and Distributed in Great Britain in 1999
by
Poyntington Publishing Company
The Lindens
Poyntington
Dorset
DT9 4LF
Telephone: 01963-220686

Set in 11/15pt Monotype Sabon
Origination by Colorhouse, Sherborne, Dorset.
Printed and bound by Jensen Press (SW) Ltd, Yeovil, Somerset.

British Library Cataloguing-in-Publication Data.
A catalogue record for this book is available from the British Library.

ISBN 0 9536697 0 X

Cover photograph: Rubambansi the Omugabe of Ankole inspecting a Guard of Honour of the Uganda Police in 1956. He is accompanied by the District Commissioner, Russel Barty, and by the OC Police, Phil Phillips.

DEDICATION

This book is dedicated to all the people who worked together in the Uganda Protectorate and who played their part in Uganda's attainment of independence. It is also written in memory of some very good friends:

Sir Walter and Lady Coutts

Gil and Betty Baird	Lionel Botcherby
Basil Branchflower	Beetle, Jack and Spadge Collins
Beadon Dening DSC	Jimmy Fleming MBE
Brian Hodges	Grace Ibingira
Frank Kalimuzo	Chris Olding
Phil and 'Mother' Phillips	George and Penny Sacker
Ken Scott	Roy Seal
Eric and Ann Weir	

GREETINGS
TO ALL THE PEOPLE OF UGANDA IN THE NEW MILLENNIUM

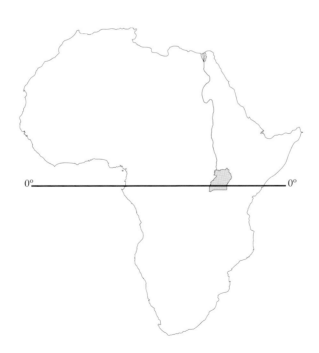

"Uganda is the pearl"
WINSTON CHURCHILL

ACKNOWLEDGEMENTS

To His Majesty the Kabaka of Buganda Ronald Muwenda Mutebi II for his permission to include a quotation from *Desecration of my Kingdom* by Sir Edward Mutesa II.

To Lord Rennell for permission to include an extract from *Frank Rhodes – a Memory*, written by his grandfather, James Rennell Rodd, for private circulation in 1905.

To Elizabeth Kanyogonya, Special Assitant for Literary Affairs to HE The President of Uganda for her advice and encouragement.

To John Symons for his suggestion that I should record these years in a series of letters.

To Deryke Belshaw, Professor Emeritus, University of East Anglia, for his comments and corrections.

To Hubert Allen, Honorary Senior Research Fellow, University of Birmingham, for his careful reading of the final draft and suggestions for its improvement.

To Sandy Dunbar for permission to reproduce his map of the Ruwenzori.

To Carolyn Reid for her work as editor.

To Curtis Brown Ltd, London, on behalf of the Estate of Sir Winston Churchill, for permission to reproduce quotations from *My African Journey*.

To Punch Ltd for permission to reproduce the quotation from Elspeth Huxley's, 'Kings and Commoners'.

To the Public Records Office for retrieving British Government records from which quotations have been included in this book.

To © Times Newspapers Limited 1997 for permission to reproduce an extract dated 1 July 1997.

To © Ferdinand Mount/Times Newspapers Limited 1999 for permission to reproduce an extract dated 13 June 1999.

To the other publishers (indicated by * in the Bibliography) who, as required and where possible, have also given their permission for other quotations.

To Andrew Johnstone, Malcolm Yesson, Richard Sercombe, Peter Langrick and Steve Clark at Colorhouse, Sherborne, Dorset for their skill in origination.

To Robin Elliot and Jensen Press (SW), Yeovil, Somerset for the production of this book.

Most of all to Mavora, my wife, for all her encouragement, advice, the design of the jacket, choice of photographs and typing and editing seemingly endless drafts and the final disc. If only we had met in the 1950s – she would have been such a wonderful District Officer's wife.

LETTERS FROM A DISTRICT OFFICER

UGANDA

WHITE NILE

MOYO

WEST NILE

ACHOLI

ARUA

GULU

KARAMOJA

MOROTO

MURCHISON FALLS

VICTORIA NILE

LIRA

LANGO

TESO

MOUNT DEBASIEN

BUNYORO

L. KYOGA

SOROTI

LAKE ALBERT

HOIMA

BUGISU

MOUNT ELGON

EAST MENGO

MUBENDE

VICTORIA NILE

BUSOGA

TERINYI FERRY

BUDAKA

MBALE

WEST MENGO

BUKEDI

FORT PORTAL

RUWENZORI

TORO

MUBENDE

KINGDOM OF BUGANDA

OWEN FALLS DAM

MUKONO

TORORO

JINJA

KILEMBE

KASESE

KAMPALA

L. GEORGE

IBANDA

BUTENGA

ENTEBBE

LAKE EDWARD

KATUNGURU

QE NATIONAL PARK

KIRUHURU

MASAKA

LAKE VICTORIA

SANGA

ANKOLE

MASAKA

SESE ISLANDS

MBARARA

KIGEZI

KIKAGATI

R. KAGERA

0 10 20 30 40 50
MILES

KISORO

KABALE

MF/RS

INTRODUCTION

In the very heart of Africa, not far from the source of the White Nile and the Mountains of the Moon, the sun's early rays captured the first smoke curls rising through the thatched roofs of homesteads hidden among the trees and plantations. Carrying their green bananas on their heads and herding their goats, local farmers and their wives walked barefoot along the dusty footpaths and tracks leading to the market place at Budaka. This was no ordinary market day. Word had spread that Balaki Kirya, described by some as a freedom fighter and by others as a rabble rouser, was coming to hold a public meeting, his first since the end of his six months' banishment from his homeland, Bukedi District in eastern Uganda – a British Protectorate.

Kirya had been punished for his part in fomenting the riots which broke out suddenly in January 1960 and which continued sporadically for six days. In all, 15 people were killed and many chiefs were driven from their houses by angry crowds which then razed some of their headquarters to the ground. A district officer, Frank Gibson, was beaten and chased by a mob. Nearly 2,000 people were arrested. Some of the rioters later fled up into the foothills of Mount Elgon and were pursued by a detachment of The King's African Rifles led by Sergeant Idi Amin, that is until he asked Jimmy Fleming, the Provincial Courts Adviser and a former officer in The Black Watch, to take command. All this strife began with the people's protests against the latest graduated tax assessments.

Subsequently a Commission of Inquiry found that the deaths and damage "must be laid at Mr Kirya's door"[1] even though he had been in India when the riots broke out. The Commission recommended that the three extra district officers, who had been posted into the area to restore law and order, should be retained for duty for some 12 months; and should continue to live in chiefs' houses in the villages rather than at district headquarters. One, given the nickname 'Smiling Teeth' by the local people, was still based in the large modern chief's house in Budaka, only a quarter of a mile from the market place. He and his colleagues practised direct rule by central government as they sought to re-establish the authority of the Bukedi Local Government and to train new chiefs to replace those killed in the riots or dismissed for incompetence. The Commission added that the extra district officers "should be without offices to ensure that they do not complain of being tied to routine."[2]

There was certainly no danger of dull routine as Kirya made his demands. "That white man must go. Why should he still be living in your chief's house here in Budaka?" Kirya was a particularly close associate of Milton Obote, the leader of the Uganda People's Congress, and was known to be an ambitious man who, with the forthcoming elections to the legislative council in view, claimed to be an expert in debating. He had told the Commission of Inquiry that "I will be one of the big bosses"[3]; it was doubtful if he was an equal expert in democracy.

Kirya knew that, on market day, hundreds would gather around the fly-encircled mud-and-wattle butchers' stalls, situated across the dusty road from the Asians' shops built of concrete and corrugated iron. Here Africans worked away at Singer sewing machines on verandas in front of open wooden doors. These were adorned with rusty advertisements for Aspro, Coca-Cola and other necessities. Inside were hoes, sugar, salt and lengths of brightly patterned cotton material for women's dresses, alongside rolls of khaki drill, the standard cloth for men's shirts and shorts.

As Kirya spoke, Uganda was on the brink of self-government and independence. Understandably in all these circumstances, his rhetoric rose to fever pitch as he demanded the white man's removal from Budaka. "Why should he fly the Union Jack at our chief's house?" 'Smiling Teeth' had by then been living in the house for some seven months, initially with a colleague but alone for the last two months. The flag, a small one and now worn by the winds, was not normally flown outside district headquarters. In this case it served to signal the Protectorate Government's determination to restore law and order. This had nearly been achieved by the time of Kirya's return to the district. The damaged chiefs' houses and offices had been rebuilt, the rules for the collection of taxes modified, some chiefs dismissed and some new ones appointed. Significantly, a levy had been raised and collected to pay for the damage. In these cost-conscious circumstances Balaki Kirya failed, fortunately, to rekindle the aggressive passions of the people. The crowd, amidst much shouting and hullabaloo, gradually dispersed. The sergeant in charge of the six policemen, who had observed the meeting at a discreet distance, reported to the occupant of the chief's house that all was well.

Instead of leading the mob across the wide veranda of my temporary house, Balaki Kirya came by my invitation to tea the next day – for I was the man with the smiling teeth! Perhaps somewhat mischievously, if not triumphantly, I had replaced the worn and tattered flag with a larger new one. Kirya did not comment, nor did he repeat his demands for my departure. As we sat with our tea on the veranda, we looked down the avenue of jacaranda and bougainvillea which I had planted, with the help of prisoners from the nearby gaol, to commemorate Her Royal Highness The Princess Margaret's wedding to Antony Armstrong-Jones. In the distance we saw fields of cotton planted for cash by local farmers. However, Kirya was intent on a richer harvest: power. He wanted to know exactly when the British would grant independence, why and how they had come to Uganda and why I had joined the Colonial Administrative Service.

Now, I seek to answer all these questions in this series of retrospective letters to a friend and fellow Cambridge geographer, Deryke Belshaw, Professor Emeritus of Development Studies at the University of East Anglia; he has lived and worked in both eastern and southern Africa. The letters reflect the role of the British in Uganda, and they outline the history of the country in the 68 years between the declaration of the Protectorate in 1894 and the granting of independence in 1962. They record the creation of a constitution with variable elements of federalism to accommodate the aspirations of some 20 different peoples, derived from three racial groups, living in four kingdoms and ten districts. They provide some insight into one example of British colonial rule and they attempt to explain why a country described by Stanley as the 'Pearl of Africa' (according to Captain Frederick Lugard's recollection)[4] came later to be almost destroyed by the regime of Idi Amin and the subsequent civil war between 1971 and 1986. Lastly, and most importantly, the letters draw attention to President Museveni's reconstruction of Uganda, as it prepares to celebrate its thirty-seventh anniversary of independence in 1999, almost on the eve of the new millennium.

---

[1] Bennett *Report of Commission of Inquiry into Disturbances in the Eastern Province* 58
[2] Ibid 37
[3] Ibid 55
[4] Lugard *The Rise of our East African Empire* Vol 2, 3

1: A JOURNEY UP A BEANSTALK

ADEN
13th August 1955

"You have been allocated Uganda." The brevity and most exciting expansiveness of these words in a telegram from the Colonial Office in March 1954 continues to fuel my imagination. As Winston Churchill wrote in 1908, "Uganda is a fairy tale. You climb up a railway instead of a beanstalk, and at the end there is a wonderful new world. The scenery is different, the vegetation is different, the climate is different, and, most of all, the people are different from anything elsewhere to be seen in the whole range of Africa."[1] It is almost as though everything will be mine when I arrive at the top of the beanstalk!

Already, there is so much to tell you. As you know, in my 24 years I had never left our shores and already I have crossed the Bay of Biscay, sailed around the Mediterranean and traversed the Red Sea. In a week or so I shall be in the heart of Africa, beginning a three-year tour of duty. Before I left home I had to explain to many friends and relations that Uganda, which was declared a British Protectorate in June 1894, is on the equator; almost at the centre of the continent. Most were surprised to hear how small it is. It is about the same size as the United Kingdom, some 94,000 square miles, but the population at present numbers only just over 5 million, the vast majority of whom are African; there are also some 48,000 Asians and 5,600 Europeans.

The last days at home were full of excitement at the prospect of the journey, which began when the hired Daimler arrived at our house in New Malden at midday on Thursday 28th July. As my luggage was strapped to the rack above the rear bumper, I took a last look around the home and garden where I had lived since 1939, except for a few months in the war when we were expelled by the explosion of a German 'doodlebug' which unfortunately killed one of our neighbours. My parents, who did not own a car, used to hire a large Austin for family holidays when all six of us departed for at least a month to a bungalow at Selsey Bill. This time they knew that I would soon be far out to sea beyond that landmark, for the Daimler was to take us to Liverpool Street Station for the first part of my long journey by railway, ship and railway 'up the beanstalk'.

We drove along the familiar Kingston by-pass where I used to wait for hours to see The King and Queen returning to London from the Epsom races, with the royal standard flying from the roof of their limousine. We passed Raynes Park Grammar School where our Shakespearean plays were reviewed in *The Times* and our motto adapted from Karl Marx urged 'to each his need, from each his power'. In Mr Gibb's geography lessons I enjoyed learning about the world and its peoples. My enthusiasm for working overseas owed much to the experience of relatives who came to see us when on leave from their work in the Malay States, Ceylon and the Gold Coast. All that they had to say was so exciting, compared to the humdrum lives of many in New Malden who commute daily from the neighbourhood to Waterloo railway terminus and the offices in the City beyond. My uncles were engineers and planters, but they told me about the work of district officers. You will remember that in each of our years at Cambridge I attended lectures on the Colonial Administrative Service given by officers on leave, who described the work both in the bush and at headquarters. (Out in the districts junior administrative officers are known as district officers or assistant district commissioners. At headquarters they are usually designated as assistant secretaries.) My keenness survived a rather blunt reply to my first letter to the Colonial Office. An official, on behalf of the Secretary of State, Oliver Lyttelton (now Lord Chandos), asked me to furnish brief particulars of my qualifications and experience so that he "could advise me as to whether any useful purpose would be served by inviting me to complete a formal application for appointment." Fortunately, when I showed you this letter you pointed out that the writer had at least addressed me as "Sir" and concluded, "Your obedient servant."

After a while the Daimler carried us over the main south-western railway line, through Putney and, at my request, past the Colonial Office at Sanctuary Buildings in Great Smith Street and then into the heart of London. I looked across the Thames at Westminster to the site of the 1951 Festival of Britain, where you and I witnessed the lowering of the Union Jack on the last night. My father, ever practical, is worried at the prospect that my career might end sooner than expected, with the lowering of the Union Jack in Uganda. I think I told you that progress towards independence was one of the issues on which I had to offer some thoughts when I attended my final Board at the Colonial Office nearly 18 months ago. It was not easy to steer a course between the Scylla of championing the 800 years which we have passed in the pursuit of democracy and the Charybdis of advocating, as some do, the premature abdication of our responsibilities in Africa or elsewhere. Somehow I must have matched Lord Chandos' thoughts which he expressed earlier this year: "There is no quicker way of putting the clock back than by putting it forward too quickly."[2] Not all the Board members were Colonial Office or civil service staff. One was a trade union official and the Board explored my willingness to work towards independence, irrespective of my own ambition. The questions also covered my capacity to occupy my spare time. I mentioned my interests in photography, music and hill-walking.

Whatever happens it seems reasonable to expect that I shall be away from London for many years and I am happy to have left it behind. I shall miss evenings at Covent Garden, where as a schoolboy I was captivated for ever by the drama, music and spectacle of *Boris Godunov*. But on the day of my departure there was little time for regret as I arrived at Liverpool Street where we were joined by my younger sister Ann, a nurse at St Mary's Hospital, Paddington. On the platform I introduced my parents to the five other cadets going with me to Uganda. (We are designated district officer cadets until our appointments are confirmed; hopefully in two years' time.) There were others going to Kenya and Tanganyika. We had all attended the one-year Colonial Office 'Devonshire' training course at Oxford and have learnt something of our colonial history, law, economics, land use and anthropology; also elementary road and house building. My Uganda-bound colleagues and I studied Luganda, the language of the Baganda, the people of the wealthy Kingdom of Buganda which lies in the centre of the Protectorate. The course was named after the tenth Duke of Devonshire who chaired a committee which met in 1946 to revise training courses for the Service; the first course had been held as early as 1927. Now the boat-train was waiting to take us to the *SS Kenya Castle* in the King George V dock. Inter-family introductions took the edge off fond family farewells. I fear my parents were sad to see me go, but they never sought to persuade me to pursue a more prosaic career. At least my brother Ronald is likely to remain in England, in the Lake District, where he has just been appointed a curate in the diocese of Carlisle. You have met my father several times; he is still the Establishment Officer for Surrey County Council. Swiftly the train pulled my colleagues and me away on our journey to East Africa. In the event there were no tears, only cheery waves. We passed through the east end of London and then towards the dockside buildings.

Suddenly, through large warehouse doors, we saw the shining lavender and white sides of the *Kenya Castle*. She is one of the more modern Union Castle line ships – 17,000 tons with one smoke-stack for her diesel engines. We went quickly up the gangway to discover our quarters; as we were very junior, these were on the lowest decks and without portholes.

Luggage stowed, the ship left the dockside and was soon nudged and tugged through the great gates and out into the running tide. Away we went down the Thames, meandering between the cranes, the river and sky tinged with pink, save for our sweeping silvery wake and the blue-grey smoky wisps from the riverside chimneys. The sun set over London.

Dinner received scant attention, even though the choice of dishes – for one raised on a ration book – was mouth-watering. We took our drinks on deck and toasted each other with thoughts of our futures in Africa. The next day we passed Selsey Bill and sailed on towards Gibraltar, the first of six ports of call on the voyage. At each of these, dockers loaded and unloaded cargo and we took the opportunity to see the various hinterlands. At 'Gib' we made the compulsory climb to see the apes. Then we were into the warmth of the Mediterranean. We could not resist a coach trip along the coast from Marseilles to view the glistening beaches and oiled skins, some of which, we were told in almost hushed tones, might be topless. We were disappointed but, east of Genoa, we found Portofino, surely the most sensuous place one could ever expect to see.

Safely through the Straits of Messina, between the real Scylla and Charybdis, we steamed on 'up the beanstalk' to Egypt and Port Said. There I met my elder sister Margaret and we had a greasy breakfast among potted palms on the dusty terrace of a small hotel just outside the docks. She is serving in Queen Alexandra's Royal Army Nursing Corps in the Canal Zone, where British troops are now guarding the canal in accordance with the Anglo-Egyptian Treaty of Friendship and Alliance of 1936. The British Government is still one of the most important owners of the canal, having bought £4 million worth of shares from the bankrupt Ismail Pasha in 1875. The Treaty is due to expire in two years' time and the canal, which was opened in 1869, will become the Egyptians' sole property in 1967.

Margaret and I had time after breakfast to take a horse-drawn carriage drive around the town. This ended with an inevitable haggle over the cost with the driver and I then rejoined the *Kenya Castle*. We moved slowly into the canal to begin the 15-hour passage. Soon Margaret's car overtook us as she was driven back to her hospital at Fayid. The heat of the Red Sea encouraged us to take salt tablets and to sleep at night on the comfortable deck chairs, in preference to our bunk beds in the stuffy cabins. Our languid days were spent lying around the swimming pool listening to the music of *Salad Days* on Edward Cunningham's portable record player; and we were being paid! I can almost hear your envy as I write, so take comfort from the fact that I am only on half-pay during the three-week voyage. My annual salary of £888 will be big money for a recently poor student, and poorer national service man before that!

As we approached Port Sudan I talked to an official who was due to disembark, and explained that I was on my way to begin work in Uganda. Bitter at the prospect of leaving the Sudan as independence fast approached, he questioned my sanity and forecast that I would be "out on my neck" in a year or so. My colleagues and I are already used to change. We had been recruited to the Colonial Administrative Service, part of Her Majesty's Colonial Service which was formed in 1837. Before we began the course at Oxford, the Oversea Civil Service was constituted to include the administrative, legal, medical, agricultural, educational, forestry and veterinary services, to name but a few of the 20 previously separate specialisms. I am not sure why 'Oversea' is in the singular; surely we are scattered over more than one sea? Rest assured, we are all certain we are not like those office-bound pen-pushers in Whitehall.

You will no doubt recall asking me at home whether I really expected a worthwhile career. In reply I rehearsed the Colonial Office view that the pace of political development in East Africa is well behind that of West Africa or the Sudan. The official from the Sudan could not appreciate that all of us who are newly appointed gladly accept that our task is to prepare Uganda for independence; we would not have joined the Service, nor been accepted, on any other basis. Our constitutional history lecturer at Oxford made it clear that we would be engaged in continuing the policy of nation-building that has been pursued for more than a century in the wake of the early explorers, led by John Cabot when he sailed from Bristol to Newfoundland in 1497. Centuries later, British imperial policy reacted to the demands for greater self-determination by our most advanced colonies, now peopled largely by inhabitants of British descent. Canada was the first to become a Dominion in 1867. Lord Rosebery, in 1884, was the first person to call the Empire a Commonweath of Nations. Under the Balfour Declaration of 1926 the Dominions, then including Australia, New Zealand and South Africa as well as Canada, were defined as autonomous communities within the British Empire, equal in status and united by a common allegiance to the Crown and freely associated as members of the British Commonwealth of Nations. Surprisingly, it was not until 1931 that the Statute of Westminster gave legal recognition to the *de facto* independence of the Dominions.

Whatever the future holds, my colleagues and I are attracted by Kenneth Bradley's memories of "the elephant who wondered whether he would trample on me but decided that I was not worth the effort; the alpen-glow on the glacier-hung peaks of South Georgia in a blue and golden dawn; the discovery of a tall blue flower and an ape in the folds of the Zambezi escarpment, when the flower was not supposed to exist nearer than Kenya and no apes nearer than the Congo River."[3]

Tomorrow we shall be calling at Aden. There will be time enough to go ashore and see something of Arabia, and to post this letter to you. Please keep it safely, as I am keeping my telegram from the Colonial Office – "You have been . . . allocated Uganda." I still wonder if it's true!

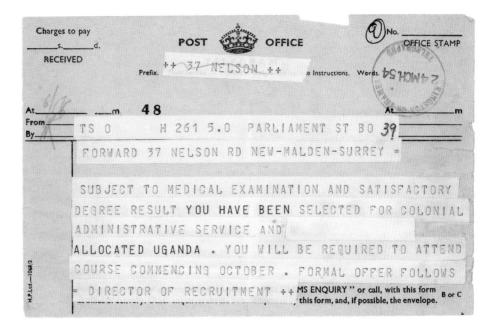

[1] Churchill *My African Journey* 86
[2] Chandos *Political Evolution in African Territories – Optima* Vol 5 No 1, 5
[3] Bradley *A Career in the Oversea Civil Service* 14

2: AROUND THE SHADOWY HORN OF GUARDAFUI

MOMBASA
18th August 1955

I am glad that I have not been posted to Aden. It may be a thriving commercial town and a busy port but the starkness of the arid scree-clad mountains which surround it is hardly welcoming. Some of those who disembarked to continue their work spoke, however, of the grandeur of the desert hinterland.

On the afternoon of our first day out from Aden we passed Cape Guardafui; its sombre and seemingly isolated outline looked grim on a cloudy day. The seas were slight but becoming rough with a heavy swell as, five hours later, we passed Ras Hafun headland. Just imagine the 4,500 miles lying to the west: the Horn of Africa, the Ethiopian mountains, the Sahara and the humid West African coast upon the Atlantic ocean. That evening we were set on a course for the equator and Mombasa. The great advantage of our leisurely progress towards our new lives is the opportunity to talk to the many on board with experience of working in Uganda; also in Kenya and Tanganyika. We would not have had this opportunity if we had flown with BOAC. It is not so long since flying boats used to land on the Nile and on Lake Victoria.

As we approached our destination, some Kenyan officials on board told us of the recent decision to withdraw armed guards from the trains between Mombasa and the Uganda border. The decision happily reflects the ending of the Mau Mau rebellion, during which British farmers and their families were murdered by trusted servants who had been forced, at fearsome ceremonies of secret oathing, to kill those whom they had served faithfully, until a night of knives and bloodshed. To our relief we were soon entertained by the comedy of 'crossing the line'. Luckily King Neptune selected others for shaving and ducking!

Once south of the equator we saw other ships bound for or leaving Mombasa. There were dhows making their way to Mogadishu, Lamu and Zanzibar. In 1859 Captain John Hanning Speke travelled from the Cape to Zanzibar aboard the corvette *Brisk*. He recorded that the corvette chased the *Manuela*, a Spanish ship suspected of slaving: she was found to have 544 slaves aboard, and "every man of the *Brisk* who first looked upon them did so with a feeling of loathing and abhorrence of such a trade. All over the vessel, but especially below, old women, stark naked, were dying in the most disgusting 'ferret box' atmosphere; while all those who had sufficient strength were pulling up the hatches, and tearing at the salt fish they found below, like dogs in a kennel."[1]   The slave trade was one of the reasons for British intervention in this part of Africa at the end of the last century: and thus our presence on these formerly blood-stained seas in the *Kenya Castle*. Although Uganda had suffered comparatively lightly, the British people in the early 1890s knew about the horrors of slavery in Africa from the speeches and writings of leaders of the anti-slavery movement: Wilberforce, Buxton and Livingstone. Uganda was part of our sphere of influence established by the Anglo-German agreement of 1890 and, as elsewhere, it was British policy to authorise a chartered company to administer new lands. Sir William Mackinnon, the founder of the Imperial British East Africa Company, petitioned for and obtained a charter in 1888. He started life as a grocer's clerk and in 40 years became the head of the British India Steamship Navigation Company. You might be interested in the attached list of some important dates in Uganda's history.

One of the first employees of the Company was Captain Frederick Lugard of the Norfolk Regiment. After service in the Afghan war of 1879-80, the Sudan campaign of 1884-85 and the Burma war of 1886-87, he applied for leave of absence and in 1888 sailed south to Africa; on half-pay like us. "I took this time a deck passage, and slept at haphazard among the timber. The necessities of the case drove me for my morning bath to the forecastle and a bucket of water among the sailors, and for my meal of broken victuals with the Italian cook, to the cook's galley alongside the engines – in the Red Sea! where the heat was such as would try a black stoker."[2]   There were none of our deck chairs for him!

In 1890 Lugard was ordered by the Company to proceed to the Kingdom of Buganda, the largest and most developed of the four kingdoms and ten districts of present-day Uganda. At that time Buganda was well organised and the Kabaka (king) and his chiefs maintained a hierarchical system of government and built well-made roads between their various headquarters. All of this must have impressed Lugard who signed treaties with Kabaka Mwanga in 1890 and in 1892. The latter prohibited the import of arms and ammunition, secured freedom to trade, abolished slave-trading and gave security to missionaries. His treaties created precedents which in later years gave the Baganda a special position in Uganda. This has always been a cause of friction between them and the Protectorate Government which has, from the earliest days, sought to develop Uganda as a unitary and African state. Two years ago the present Governor, Sir Andrew Cohen, although renowned as a progressive and liberal man, deported the present Kabaka, His Highness Frederick Mutesa II. This action followed Mutesa's support for those in his kingdom who advocated separate independence for Buganda. Although the Government in London stated that the deportation decision was final, the Protectorate Government found that Buganda could not be governed without the Kabaka and so talks have been held in London to try to resolve the crisis.

An interesting point is that Lugard could not have foreseen the effect of his treaties or of his policy of indirect rule, a system by which local rulers were encouraged to look after their own local affairs. He had but little knowledge of the territories beyond Buganda. He was also preoccupied with the religious wars that arose from the competing claims of Protestant and Catholic missionaries and their converts. These inhibited the conduct of trade and the Company was therefore unable to continue to fund his presence in Uganda. In 1892, in spite of generous help from the Church Missionary Society, it announced its intention to withdraw. There were immediate protests at home, and on his return to England Lugard led a campaign in the correspondence columns of *The Times*. Public opinion was expressed through 174 resolutions to the Foreign Office, calling for a continued British presence in Uganda. These resolutions were the product of scores of meetings throughout the country as profound concern developed about the fate of Uganda, its people, its Christian converts and the missionaries. The magazine *Punch* carried a cartoon showing Uganda as a black baby dumped in a basket on the steps of John Bull's house. Chamberlain said, "What is wanted for Uganda, is what Birmingham has got – an improvement scheme."[3] The village of South Creake in Norfolk, not far from your home, sent a petition signed by the vicar and 104 people, ten of whom were illiterate and simply put their marks. How could they have known much of Uganda? And yet they felt sufficiently moved to protest about the decision.

The resolutions emphasised a moral obligation to suppress the slave trade, and to safeguard the Christian missionaries and their converts. The British people had been shocked to hear that Bishop Hannington had been killed on the orders of Kabaka Mwanga in 1885, and that both Protestant and Catholic converts had been cruelly executed in 1886 when they refused to deny their faith. There were also concerns to further trade and commerce. The Gladstone Government, after prolonged and acrimonious debate – in which Lord Rosebery, the Foreign Secretary, threatened to resign – eventually agreed to bear the Company's costs for the first three months of 1893. Sir Gerald Portal, Consul-General in Zanzibar, was instructed to enquire and report on the future of Uganda. Rosebery gave Portal instructions to arrange the best means of administering Uganda but, in a covering note, he made it clear unofficially that "public sentiment here will expect and support the maintenance of the British sphere of influence."[4] He also commented bluntly that "as a rather one-horse Company has been able to administer the country I suppose the Empire will be equal to it."[5]

As our sea journey came to an end, I am not at all sure that I and my five colleagues really felt that we would 'be equal to it'. However, doubts were soon set aside as, after a splendid final dinner of Supreme of Turbot and Supreme of Chicken Santa Lucia, the six of us stood together on the deck. We had all been 'allocated Uganda' and we approached Mombasa at 6 o'clock on the morning of Friday 19th August, with supreme, if unjustified, confidence. The voyage of 6,773 miles had taken 22 blissful days.

Not so many years before us, in January 1893, Sir Gerald Portal had met with five good friends near Mombasa to prepare for his mission, on foot of course, to Uganda. One was his brother, Captain Raymond Portal, and another was a career diplomatist, James Rennell Rodd. Sir Gerald died on his return to England in January 1894 and four of his friends had died by 1905. Thus Sir Gerald, having recommended that the Government should maintain control over Uganda, sadly failed to live to read the Declaration of the Protectorate in *The London Gazette* on 18th June 1894. That summer Rodd, the only survivor of the six and then en poste in Stockholm, wrote a poem in memory of all five. When in Oxford I found a copy of it in *The Uganda Journal* for March 1953 and it is highly evocative of their friendship and the hazards faced by early travellers in Africa. I quote a short extract, as we too had been "light-hearted farers through the deep" and had, like them, sailed around:

> The shadowy horn of Guardafui,
> Where sudden night closed round a sea
> That drowned the old familiar stars,
> And we beheld through dripping spars
> The Southern Cross climb up the sky,
> . . .
> How all was welcome, morn and noon
> And starry eve and Afric Moon.
> As yet we had no watch to keep,
> Light-hearted farers through the deep.

The fact that so many of the administrators died in those early years may be compared with the present time when most district officers retire to claim their pensions. This is a good and welcome indication of the progress that has already been achieved in our African territories.

To us, arriving 62 years later, the coastline from a distance looked strangely unlike my vision of Africa. There were red-roofed bungalows amongst the green vegetation; we might still have been off Selsey Bill! But soon the palm trees stood out and we saw beaches of white sand unlike any in Sussex. The *Kenya Castle* moored alongside modern warehouses and was invaded by hosts of singing stevedores who quickly opened the ship's hatches, not to find salt fish or slaves, but to unload our heavy luggage, Edward Cunningham's car and all the varied imports required by the rapidly growing economies of Kenya and Uganda. Edward, who had lost part of his left leg in the Korean War, had arranged to import a car so that he would be fully mobile from the start. We wished him well, and also David Pasteur whom he had asked to accompany him on the long drive to Jinja; there Edward would have to set off northwards to Soroti, the headquarters of Teso District in the Eastern Province, leaving David to find his way to Fort Portal, the headquarters of Toro District in the west.

There is very little time for the remaining four of us to catch the train to Uganda and for me to post this letter.

[1] Speke *Journal of the Discovery of the Source of the Nile* 8
[2] Lugard *The Rise of our East African Empire* Vol 1, 3
[3] Low *The Uganda Journal* Vol 18 No 2, 97
[4] Ibid 98
[5] Ibid 98

A UGANDA CHRONOLOGY

150   Ptolomy's map shows the Mountains of the Moon and the source of the Nile.

1862   Speke discovers the source of the White Nile.

1875   Stanley meets Kabaka Mutesa I and writes letter to *The Daily Telegraph*.

1877   British missionaries arrive in Uganda.

1884   Death of Kabaka Mutesa I and the succession of Kabaka Mwanga.

1885   Bishop Hannington murdered on the orders of Kabaka Mwanga.

1886   Christian converts martyred.

1889   Kabaka Mwanga deposed.

1890   The German Karl Peters reaches Uganda and signs treaty with Kabaka Mwanga, now restored to his throne.
Anglo-German Agreement.
Lugard sent to Uganda by the Imperial British East Africa Company and signs treaty with Kabaka Mwanga.

1892   The Company announces its intention to leave Uganda.
Lugard helps pro-British Protestants defeat pro-French Catholics in Buganda and signs second treaty with Kabaka Mwanga.
British Cabinet sends Portal to report on the future of Uganda.

1893   The Company gives up responsibility for Uganda.
Portal recommends retention of Uganda by the British Governmnent.

1894   Uganda declared a British Protectorate.

1897   Attempt by Kabaka Mwanga to challenge the Protectorate Government fails.
Kabaka Mwanga deposed and succeeded by his infant son, Daudi Chwa.

1899   Capture of Kabaka Mwanga and Kabalega, the Mukama of Bunyoro, and their exile to the Seychelles.

1900   Sir Harry Johnston signs a new agreement with the Baganda.

1901   Uganda railway reaches Kisumu, Kenya.

1907   Winston Churchill visits Uganda.

1914   Daudi Chwa becomes Kabaka at the age of 18 years.

1939   Kabaka Daudi Chwa dies and is succeeded by Edward Mutesa II, aged 15 years.

1944   HE Sir Charles Dundas replaces district commissioners in Buganda with residents, having an advisory role only.

1946   Dr Edgar Worthington, Development Adviser, sets out 10-year development plan for Uganda.

1953   HE Sir Andrew Cohen deports Kabaka Mutesa II.

3: THROUGH THE COUNTRY OF THE MAN-EATING LIONS

ENTEBBE
22nd August 1955

Once ashore from the *Kenya Castle*, we really felt the warmth, clamour and friendliness of Africa for the first time, as we were guided through the crowds to a taxi and driven to Mombasa railway station. To our surprise, most of the carriages were of gleaming aluminium; they must have been recently imported. Hubert Allen and I shared one compartment, Robin Palmer and John Cleave another. After much hustle and noise upon the platform, we left the station in the late afternoon and became absorbed in the views of grass-roofed homesteads, where everyone seemed to stop to wave while they tended their fires and cooking-pots. Smoke and steam rose up to meet the descending darkness, which is complete by seven o'clock every day of the year in these equatorial parts. Then came the summons to dinner. The dining car was from another era, wood-panelled and softly lit by table lights which made our silver cutlery glisten. It was marked 'The Uganda Railway'. The waiters moved silently and barefooted, bearing bowls of brown Windsor soup. What could have been more incongruous?

There was a reluctance to retire for the first of the two nights of the final stage of our journey, now at last 'up a railway instead of a beanstalk'. It is hard to imagine that Sir Gerald Portal took only 78 days to walk 820 miles to Kampala. This was considerably less than the usual 90 days because of his efficient organisation of a 'caravan' of 400 porters and partly trained Zanzibari soldiers. But the recruitment and medical examination of porters and "the selection and purchase of provisions, of equipment, of innumerable articles of barter, such as cloth and cotton stuffs of different qualities, beads of several sizes and kinds, iron, copper, and brass wire, small chains, looking-glasses and coloured handkerchiefs, of axes, bill-hooks, intrenching tools, ropes, canvas, tents and their equipment, medical stores, and, in short, of all the thousand and one articles which may sound like trifles"[1] had to be organised in the short space of one month. Just before he set out Portal was handed some English newspapers "in which the opinion was advanced that our Mission was being despatched too late, and could not possibly arrive in Uganda before the evacuation of that country by the Company; that in consequence we should find on our arrival nothing but disorder, anarchy, and bloodshed, should probably have to fight for our lives, and that a strong military expedition would be needed to get us out again! My last official act before starting was, therefore, to send a telegram to HM Secretary of State, hazarding the prophecy that we should cross the Nile and enter Uganda on or about the 13th of March."[2] In the event Sir Gerald and his brother celebrated their arrival on that day by fishing at the Ripon Falls on the Nile; so much for the speculation of journalists!

The impetus for the railway came from the anti-slave trade conference in Brussels in November 1889. This followed 50 years in which the European maritime powers, particularly ourselves, had tried to check the sea-borne slave trade. The conference concluded in a General Act which called for protectorates to be established in the interior of Africa, and the construction of roads and, in particular, of railways. After much debate in the House of Commons, the sum of £20,000 was voted in 1892 to meet the costs of a preliminary survey which had been started in late 1891. There were "five years of excoriating parliamentary debate"[3] before the first rails were laid at Mombasa in 1896; they reached Nairobi in May 1899. When Winston Churchill, then Parliamentary Under-Secretary for the Colonies, took his place in 1907 upon an ordinary garden seat fastened onto the cow-catcher of a locomotive he recorded, "here is a railway like the British Fleet, 'in being' – not a paper plan, or an airy dream but an iron fact grinding along through the jungle and the plain, waking with its whistles the silences of the Nyanza, and startling the tribes out of their primordial nakedness with 'Americani' piece goods *made in Lancashire*."[4] It was very hard for us to realise the short time in which all this had been achieved. Churchill was surprised by the sophistication of Nairobi society in 1908: "the ball given by the Governor to celebrate the King's birthday revealed a company gay with uniforms, and ladies in pretty dresses, assembled upon a spot where scarcely ten years before lions hunted undisturbed."[5]

Throughout that first evening the train steadily but slowly carried us away from the humid coast. The cooler drier atmosphere was welcome as we progressed through valleys and gorges towards the Tsavo river and grasslands inhabited by wild animals, notably lion, whose forebears had not been averse to eating some of the builders for breakfast. One man-eater actually opened the sliding door of an inspection carriage in 1900. The door subsequently closed, due to the gradient of the line, and the lion seized the superintendent of the railway police who had fallen asleep while guarding two colleagues. It carried him out of a window and into the bush! With such stories in our minds we pulled the door of our compartment tightly shut and eventually went to sleep.

We were awake early, scanning the country for a sight of big game, disappointingly without success. Our breakfast brought a new taste; paw-

paw with lime juice gave us an appetite for eggs and bacon. Our effortless progress continued, albeit as slowly as before. Then our locomotive gathered pace as it crossed the Athi plains on the way into Nairobi. Hubert has an aunt living in the city and she took us to her home in Hurlingham Road where she lives with her mother. On the way Aunt Priscilla showed us part of the city centre. She pointed out modern hotels for tourists and a variety of stores for the farming settlers. These were surrounded by countless shops in the bazaar which appeared to stock everything one could possibly need. Most of them are owned by Asians, some of whom may well be descendants of those who built the railway. Priscilla is the librarian at the Medical Research Laboratory and in her spare time is the secretary of the East African Natural History Society. Her mother's bungalow, with shaded verandas, was comfortable and very English, except for her houseboy, who padded softly around the lunch table in his ankle-length white kanzu (gown), red cummerbund and red fez.

After lunch some of us began to fidget and wonder when we should go back to the station. Eventually Hubert let us know that we could linger a while as his aunt planned to drive us up to the next station at Limuru; the train takes much longer to climb from Nairobi to the edge of the Rift Valley at a height of over 6,000 feet above sea level. We duly overtook the train and were soon aboard again, descending the Kikuyu escarpment. "As the train claws its way downwards by slant and zigzag along its face, a majestic panorama breaks upon the view. Far below, bathed in sunshine, stretching away to misty purple horizons, lie the broad expanses of the Rift Valley. Its level surface is broken by strangely moulded volcanic hills and shattered craters. The opposite mountain wall looms up in the far distance, brown and blue. We gaze down upon the plain as from a balloon, mistaking forests for patches of green grass, and mighty trees for thorn-scrub."[6] As we progressed across the valley we saw flamingos on Lake Nakuru and when dusk came the train approached the seemingly impassable western escarpment. The builders of the track had worked miracles and in the night we climbed to Timboroa at 9,136 feet, the highest railway station in the Empire, before the long descent through Eldoret towards Tororo, the first stop in Uganda – and the sudden prospect of real work after weeks of idleness!

Uganda is divided administratively into four provinces, Buganda and the Eastern, Northern and Western Provinces; the latter three are headed by provincial commissioners. I need to add quickly that the Kingdom of Buganda, which covers over a quarter of the land area of Uganda and contains more than a quarter of the total population, is not on the same footing as the other provinces. It is mostly referred to as a kingdom rather than as a province. This is because the Buganda Government, largely for historical and geographical reasons, has greater powers than the other local governments in Uganda. The Resident in Kampala is the equivalent of a provincial commissioner but he is in many ways more an adviser than an administrator. There are four districts in each of the three provinces. To make matters more complicated three districts in the Western Province – Ankole, Bunyoro and Toro – are also kingdoms, but their rulers have comparatively little power and their homelands are not usually referred to as kingdoms. We had been notified at Mombasa of our postings to six different districts, two of us to each of the Eastern, Northern and Western Provinces. So, Hubert Allen and John Cleave left the train at Tororo and awaited another to take them northwards towards Gulu and Moroto, the headquarters of Acholi and Karamoja Districts in the Northern Province. In Karamoja the people, who are livestock herders, drink a mixture of blood and milk and have yet to become accustomed to wearing clothes.

On leaving Tororo Robin and I travelled through Bukedi District and then entered Busoga District, the home of the Basoga people who speak Lusoga. Lusoga is not unlike Luganda, the language of the Baganda, which we had all been taught at Oxford, even though none of us will be posted to Buganda until we have some experience. Luganda is, however, understood by most of the people who live in the southern half of Uganda. It would have been impossible to give each of us separate language training because there are some 20 languages in Uganda, reflecting the number of different peoples who severally belong to three distinct ethnic groups: the Bantu, Nilotic and Nilo-Hamitic peoples. We tried to practice our Luganda upon the cheerful Basoga who greeted us with fruit and eggs for sale at every station. It was perhaps not surprising that much of our efforts to talk to them fell on uncomprehending ears. Eventually we arrived at Jinja, the headquarters of Busoga District; and Robin left the train. Then there was one!

After Jinja the railway crosses the Nile by a bridge which was not completed until 1931. It was disappointing to find that I only had a limited view of the nearby Owen Falls hydro-electric dam because the railway bridge, which we crossed very slowly, is upstream of the dam, nearer to Lake Victoria. Originally the bridge carried a roadway below the rails but this disappeared beneath the waters when the dam was completed. This was partly because the dam was built three feet higher than had been originally planned for the generation of electricity in order to meet the irrigation needs of the Egyptian Government. (The area of Lake Victoria is about the same as that of Scotland; so the Egyptians, who paid for the cost of the extra height, achieved a bargain in terms of their irrigation requirements.)

The so-called Uganda railway terminated at Kisumu in Kenya for many years; until 1931 earlier travellers, such as Winston Churchill, reached Uganda after crossing the north-eastern part of Lake Victoria by steamship. When Churchill was taken to see the Ripon Falls, which Speke had identified as the source of the Nile, on 28th July 1862 he wrote, "So much power running to waste, such a coign of vantage unoccupied, such a lever to control the natural forces of Africa ungripped, cannot but vex and stimulate imagination. And what fun to make the immemorial Nile begin its journey by diving through a turbine!"[7] Speke named the Ripon Falls after the first Marquess of Ripon who had been President of the Royal Geographical Society when Speke was preparing for his expedition.

You probably remember the many reports in the press in April last year when Her Majesty The Queen opened the Owen Falls Dam and fulfilled Churchill's vision. The name of these falls was first recorded on Lt Col JRL Macdonald's 1 inch:10 miles 'Map of Uganda' of 1899-1900. It is likely that Macdonald used the name of Major E Roderick Owen, a colleague, because Owen had crossed the Nile near Jinja on his way to and from Buganda. I assume that this must be the Roddy Owen who was one of Sir Gerald Portal's five companions in 1893. There is no evidence that Owen discovered the falls. "Nevertheless there is an incidental appositeness in this name: for Owen was, for a short time in 1884, aide-de-camp to the very Marquess of Ripon, then Viceroy of India, who is commemorated by the adjacent Ripon Falls."[8]

And so I neared the end of the 'beanstalk' as the train, once across the bridge, entered the Kingdom of Buganda on its way to Kampala, the commercial centre of Uganda and the capital of Buganda. At the same time David Pasteur was making his way by road to Toro District in the Western Province. David is particularly pleased, as a mountaineer of some repute, since the fabled Mountains of the Moon, more prosaically called the Ruwenzori Mountains, will be in his sights. Astride the equator, their snow-capped peaks occasionally emerge from their mantle of clouds. I have been told that they can sometimes be seen from Mbarara in Ankole District, my destination in the south of the Western Province. Meanwhile, still in Buganda, I noticed more signs of progress. Houses are almost invariably roofed with corrugated iron, and the roads run straight between lush small coffee farms. I had glimpses of extensive Asian-owned sugar estates and prosperous small towns. Cars, markets and the imposing headquarters of Buganda Government chiefs at Mukono heralded my approach to Kampala.

I was met at the station by one of the Establishment Secretary's staff and she first drove through the outskirts of Kampala on well-maintained tarmac roads past shops and new housing. This area was once a swamp where the residents of Kampala used to shoot duck. My new mentor promised me that I would have the chance to visit Kampala before departing up country on Tuesday. Then by way of a large roundabout, with an imposing clock tower at its centre, we began the 22-mile journey to Entebbe, the administrative capital of Uganda. The tarmac road ran across low-lying swampy areas between a series of flat-topped hills, on the slopes of which the local farmers produce an abundance of green bananas, coffee, and a variety of fruits and vegetables. The countryside exudes fertility and the sky burns with its blueness, yet the average temperature remains constant between 70° and 80°F throughout the year. I was taken directly to the Lake Victoria Hotel, a modern building set in gardens full of canna lilies and separated from the lake by the lush greens and fairways of a golf course. It hardly seems at the moment as if I am in 'darkest Africa', but then "Uganda is the pearl"![9]

Unlike my five colleagues, who had proceeded directly to their districts, I was asked to call at the Ministry of Local Government in the morning. Meanwhile, it being Sunday, I rested, continued this letter and made the most of the hotel's magnificent meals.

Today I was briefed on recent developments. The pace of political change has accelerated, even while we were on the high seas. First, a transitional agreement was signed by the Governor and three personal representatives of the Kabaka on 15th August. This agreement will pave the way for His Highness's return as a constitutional ruler on 17th October. Secondly, the Protectorate Government has just been reorganised by the introduction of a ministerial system. There are eleven ministers; six of whom are government officials; five non-officials (three Ugandans, an Asian and a European) have also become ministers. One of the Uganda ministers is the Hon ZCK Mungonya who, I am told, was formerly the head of the Ankole Local Government. Changes to the Legislative Council have been made; half the members are now Africans. You may not think this is sufficient, but note that the first African member was not appointed until 1945, 51 years after the declaration of the Protectorate. Thirdly, a new district administration ordinance has been passed by the Council. This will transfer substantial powers and responsibilities to local authorities. I was pleased to hear that Ankole is well on the way to being the first district council to be proclaimed under the ordinance.

Later I was driven into Kampala for some shopping. There is little doubt that I shall be able to obtain most of my housekeeping requirements quite easily and I understand that I shall be able to have my khaki uniforms made to measure in Mbarara. On my return to the hotel I went to the gateway of Government House to sign His Excellency the Governor's visitors book. This is done as a mark of respect when people arrive in the country at Entebbe. They sign again when they depart, adding the letters '*ppc*' – meaning *pour prendre congé*: to take one's leave. Government House is approached by a curving, rising road and I was shown through the gates and into a room next to the guard room by the policemen on duty. As I entered the grounds I saw a fine mansion, its cream-washed walls below terracotta-tiled roofs set in extensive gardens. The Governor's standard, a Union Jack with Uganda's emblem of a crested crane in a wreath at the centre, was flying from an immensely high flagpole beyond the lawns to show that Sir Andrew Cohen was in residence.

A glimpse of Government House seen from near the guard room.

It is now evening and tomorrow I shall be driven up to Mbarara, the headquarters of Ankole District. Meanwhile the cicadas are beginning to buzz shrilly around the verandas and courtyards of this comfortable hotel. Am I really in Uganda? Yes I am: I have just seen what looks like a small lizard walking upside down across the ceiling. It is so transparent that I can see its guts – there was nothing like that in New Malden!

[1] Portal *The British Mission to Uganda in 1893*, 7
[2] Ibid 27
[3] Churchill *My African Journey* 5
[4] Ibid 5
[5] Ibid 21
[6] Ibid 67
[7] Ibid 132
[8] Thomas & Dale *The Uganda Journal* Vol 17 No 2, 117
[9] Churchill op cit 197

4: AMONG THE BANYANKOLE

You will be glad to know, judging from your most welcome letter and your sardonic comments on my enjoyment of half-pay and the music of *Salad Days* aboard the *Kenya Castle*, that I have been given plenty of work to do since I arrived here from Entebbe eight weeks ago.

I left the haven of the Lake Victoria Hotel on 3rd August after an early lunch when a staff car arrived punctually to bring me here to Mbarara. The driver spoke little English and did not seem to understand my Luganda! At the outskirts of Kampala we turned south-westwards on an excellent tarmac road to Masaka, a distance of 80 miles. This was built fairly recently by Stirling Astaldi, a British/Italian company, which uses massive earth-moving excavators and graders. It runs, for the most part, straight as a die over the low hills and across embankments through the swamps. Now and then I could see Lake Victoria to the east. When Speke travelled northwards to Kampala along this route, almost 100 years ago, he praised the roads which "were as broad as our coach-roads, cut through the long grasses, straight over the hills and down through the woods in the dells – a strange contrast to the wretched tracks in all the adjacent countries. The huts were kept so clean and so neat, not a fault could be found with them – the gardens the same. Wherever I strolled I saw nothing but richness, and what ought to be wealth. The whole land was a picture of quiescent beauty, with a boundless sea in the background."[1] But he had difficulties in the swamps: "one in particular, was rather large, being 150 yards wide. It was sunk where I crossed it, like a canal, 14 feet below the plain; and what with mire and water combined, so deep, I was obliged to take off my trousers whilst fording it. Once across, we sought for and put up in a village beneath a small hill, from the top of which I saw the Victoria N'yanza for the first time on this march. . . We marched on again over the same kind of ground, alternately crossing rush-drains of minor importance, though provokingly frequent, and rich gardens, from which, as we passed, all the inhabitants bolted at the sound of our drums, knowing well that they would be seized and punished."[2] Today it is possible to drive from Kampala to Masaka in the time that Speke probably took to cross a couple of these swamps; and without taking off one's trousers!

At Masaka we paused for a short break and the driver refuelled the car. I had time to see that the town looked very prosperous; lorries were numerous and the shops, mainly owned by Asians, were well stocked. As in Kenya, many of their ancestors may have come to East Africa to work on the railway. The journey from Masaka westwards to Mbarara is another 80 miles or so. The tarmac ends at Masaka and the road onwards is built of murram, a loose, dusty, red lateritic gravel. This material is fairly common throughout the whole country and supplies are reasonably adjacent to most roads; so you know why Speke was so impressed with the roads in his day in Buganda – and they were all built by hand! Now, the passage of vehicles creates ridges in the gravel, often four inches high and about six or so inches apart. I noticed that there is an optimum speed, about 50 miles an hour, at which the corrugations have a minimal effect upon the suspension of a car. This speed is far too fast, however, when there are pot holes ahead. Braking produces an abundance of rattles and shudders and most people therefore drive fast on the best side of the road. The rule, of course, is to drive on the left and approaching vehicles each strive to maintain the best line; the weaker driver gives way first! After about two hours we paused for a Coca-Cola at a small trading centre, Lyantonde, almost on the boundary between Buganda and Ankole.

Although not literally, I was following in the footsteps of Major Cunningham who was one of Sir Gerald Portal's staff. Shortly after the Protectorate was declared in 1894 Cunningham arrived on foot at Mbarara. Just imagine walking some 160 miles. It probably took him about two weeks compared to my one afternoon. The Protectorate had at first been restricted to Buganda but it was soon seen to be necessary that the lands to the west should also be brought under British protection. Henry Morton Stanley, the American explorer and journalist, who found David Livingstone at Ujiji in Tanganyika in 1871, had made a number of treaties with chiefs in the early years of exploration, including one with Uchunku in Ankole in 1888. Lugard made a further agreement with another Ankole chief on behalf of the Imperial British East Africa Company in 1891.

When Sir Gerald Portal was sent on his mission to Uganda in 1892 the British Foreign Office was concerned about the many treaties made by the Company. This was expressed as follows. "One particular difficulty is inherent in the situation. The Company has of late concluded a great number of treaties with native chiefs including one of perpetual friendship with Mwanga which last however had not been ratified by the Secretary of State. There are many others (eighty-three in all) which have been so approved. Whether an approval of this kind can be held in any way, directly or indirectly, to bind HMG is a moot point. (Blue Book Africa, number 1, 1893)"[3]

The originals of some of the Company's treaties are kept among the records at Entebbe. The Company certainly made comprehensive claims in return for its offer of protection:

LET IT BE KNOWN to all whom it may concern that .... has placed himself and all his Territories, Countries, Peoples, and Subjects under the protection, rule and government of the IMPERIAL BRITISH EAST AFRICA COMPANY, and has ceded to the said Company all his sovereign rights and rights of government over all his Territories, Countries, Peoples, and Subjects, and that the said Company have assumed the said rights so ceded to them as aforesaid, and that the said Company hereby grant their protection and the benefit of their rule and government to Him, his Territories, Countries, Peoples, and Subjects, and hereby authorise him to use the Flag of the said Company as a sign of their protection.

Dated at ....this ......day of .... 18....

(Signed) ....

On behalf of the Imperial British East Africa Company.[4]

You may not find it surprising that Sir Gerald reported to the Foreign Office later in 1893 that, "whether rightly or wrongly, the impression conveyed to the different native chiefs and peoples in this region when they signed treaties and received the Company's flag and promise of protection, was that they were thereby placing themselves under the protection of the Government of Great Britain."[5] Portal, mindful of this situation and of Rosebery's unofficial note, advised the British Government to retain control of Uganda.

It must therefore have been Cunningham's task to make an official agreement with the Omugabe of Ankole. In spite of the Omugabe's unwillingness to meet Cunningham a treaty was signed by the Nganzi, the Omugabe's adviser, and Cunningham on 29th August 1894. This proliferation of treaties ended on 30th June 1896 with the extension of the Protectorate to the eastern and western parts of what is now Uganda.

We continued westwards and the road twisted and turned through low hills and grassy plains peppered with giant anthills, some 12 feet high or so. The savannah grasslands were greened by the rains which have been falling steadily since the dry season of June and July. We frequently saw the distinctive Ankole cattle which have immense horns, six feet or so apart at their tips. We passed a small village called Sanga which, according to the driver, used to be well known for its man-eating lions! Then, in a little while, I saw ahead a wide and open plain edged in the far distance by low rounded hills, their sides etched with scrub-filled valleys. There, in the middle, I saw the white-walled buildings and shining roofs of Mbarara, my new home.

I had been told in Entebbe that Ankole is one of the most beautiful and progressive districts in Uganda, with a population of around 400,000 in its 6,000 square miles. To the south it borders Tanganyika and Ruanda-Urundi, and it bestrides the equator in the north. The climate is usually very pleasant as much of the district lies between 4,000 and 8,000 feet above sea level. Mbarara is situated just below 5,000 feet and the weather is usually hot by day and cool by night, a kind of perpetual English summer. As we drove into the town I saw that most of the shops lining the main murram road are owned by Asians and are built of concrete blocks and roofed with corrugated iron. Each has its veranda to accommodate one or two tailors, who I am told will stitch together my khaki uniform in no time at all. We drew up outside a bar in the main street; its swing doors might have come from America's wild west. As the dust settled the sun sank in a brief but beautiful moment. Choking in the dust I wondered whether I was going to enjoy Mbarara; it seemed to have the atmosphere of a one-horse town! I was the centre of considerable attention but we were soon given directions to the District Commissioner's house. Continuing along the main road I noticed that kerb stones had been installed, perhaps to separate future tarmac from the embryonic pavements. We navigated a roundabout formed by upturned culvert pipes and white painted lumps of rock, all of which, like the modern Shell petrol station, had a thorough coating of reddish dust. I was soon relieved to find that the official houses in Mbarara are set amidst trees bordering a golf course and we drove up the long drive to the house; its cool wide verandas were a most welcome sight.

Eric Weir and his wife Ann welcomed me warmly and invited me in for a drink. He is an experienced District Commissioner, or DC in everyday speech. They suggested that I should move into the Ankole Hotel straight away as I would have to take my turn in waiting for a house. Eric told me that I would find Sir George Duntze, the Provincial Commissioner, and his wife staying there. After a while I was driven round the golf course to find the hotel, little more than a collection of thatched round huts, known as rondavels, sited around the dining and sitting rooms, built of brick columns, with trellis work and rush matting forming some of the walls. I was greeted on the creeper-clad veranda by the owner, a tall, portly and autocratic Englishwoman, Blanche Hall. Her husband, now retired, had been one of the early tin and beryl miners in the south of the district. The Provincial

The long-horned Ankole cattle, the prized possessions of the Bahima pastoralists.

Commissioner, usually referred to as the PC, was on one of his routine visits to Mbarara. He invited me to join him and Lady Duntze for coffee after dinner. Sir George welcomed me to Western Province which consists of Bunyoro, Kigezi and Toro Districts, in addition to Ankole. Here the hereditary ruler is Rubambansi Charles Godfrey Gasyonga II, the Omugabe of Ankole. In Bunyoro and Toro each ruler is known as Omukama. Kigezi has no traditional ruler. Sir George explained that these rulers are far more co-operative than the Kabaka of Buganda and accept their present roles, which are already essentially those of constitutional monarchs. Kigezi, along with all the other nine non-kingdom districts in Uganda, is headed by the appointed leader of its local government.

Sir George asked me about my time in Oxford. He seemed quite interested that I had rowed for Selwyn College at Cambridge and had coached Keble College's first eight at Oxford. Unknowingly, I complained of the inadequacy of the river at Oxford, where unlike Cambridge, there is no immediate access to a good long stretch of water. There are too many locks and bends. You will be amused to know that Sir George made no comment, but I subsequently discovered that he had been awarded his Leander colours whilst he was at University College! But he did tell me that there is an annual canoe regatta for fishermen from Ankole and Toro at Katunguru on the Kazinga Channel, which joins Lake Edward and Lake George. He added that there is also a race for officials from the two districts and that he paddles for Toro, as he lives there. Lady Duntze asked me if I would have to stay in the hotel for long and I replied that the DC had told me that this was uncertain. I could not necessarily expect to move into my predecessor's house when he, David Craxton, leaves shortly as others may have a prior claim. He will have completed his first three-year tour in Ankole.

On my first day I walked up the main road from the hotel to the DC's office. This is to one side of a large grassed area in the middle of which the Union Jack flies. It is a long low building with wide verandas lined with benches, on which a number of the local people, Banyankole, were already patiently sitting. David Craxton met me. He is Assistant District Commissioner III (ADC III in everyday speech) and I shall take his place. He introduced me to Russel Barty, ADC I, who explained that Freddie Sheridan would arrive in a month's time to take up the ADC II post. David had arranged a programme for me to meet the staff at the nearby headquarters of the Ankole Local Government and the various departmental staff based in Mbarara. The Provincial Commissioner arrived and went all round the offices, greeting all the staff, before beginning talks with the DC. David then introduced me to Gil Baird, the executive officer in charge of Mbarara township. He and his wife Betty are keen to teach me to play golf. I met the chief clerk, interpreters and office boys whose names I must learn.

In the afternoon David drove me in his Peugeot car to meet the Enganzi, the leader of the Ankole Local Government, and his two senior officials. Kesi Nganwa, whose predecessors were titled Nganzi, greeted me warmly. David had coached me in the Runyankore greeting and I did my best to reproduce it. Fortunately it is not too unlike Luganda but 'l' is mainly replaced by 'r'. The Enganzi seemed pleased to see me and I was struck by his energy and sense of purpose. He is small in stature and is one of the agricultural Bairu people of Bantu origin. The Chief Justice, Alfred Mutashwera, and the Treasurer, Perezi Kanyamunyu, are Bahima; confident and tall, they are cattle owners of the Hamitic race. David told me that the Bahima are related to the Tutsi, the aristocratic minority rulers of Ruanda, part of the Belgian (ex-German) mandated territory of Ruanda-Urundi which adjoins Ankole District to the south. All of these important officials greeted me in a very encouraging way; they clearly had a good rapport with David, a graduate of the London School of Economics and some 20 years younger than themselves. They must have seen a number of raw young ADCs come and go, but there was no doubt that their welcome was genuine.

Their headquarters consists of a large meeting hall for the Eishengyero, the District Council. A porte-cochère provides protection from the rains for important visitors arriving by car. I noticed that David modestly parked elsewhere. There are also a number of stores as well as other offices and a prison. All the buildings are built in permanent materials in a simple but functional style. At every corner large cylindrical water tanks collect rain water from the extensive corrugated-iron roofs. I also met Jack Wykes, a retired public works department engineer, who had been recruited to oversee their building activities. As we left, David pointed to the Omugabe's palace set upon a nearby hill with a flagpole and open grounds in front, the whole surrounded by a traditional elephant-grass stockade. Palace might seem a rather grand description, but Jack had built the Omugabe a fine two-storey house under a tiled roof with distant views over the surrounding plains, including the humble bungalows of the British officials set around their golf course!

On other days I called on the heads of the various Protectorate Government departments working in Ankole. The Officer Commanding Police, Phil Phillips, is a man of great girth and height. He explained his triple responsibilities. As OC Police he has about 25 men under his command and these include two British inspectors. There are one or two small police stations out in the district. As OC Prisons he showed me around the prison; I thought that the inmates looked fit and well. Finally he is OC Immigration, for Ankole has frontiers with Tanganyika, Ruanda-Urundi and the Belgian Congo, across our frontage on Lake Edward.

Notice that I write 'our' frontage. I have been so well received by everyone that I feel very much at home. One weekend recently I went with David to an agricultural show at Kichwamba on the edge of an escarpment overlooking the Queen Elizabeth National Park. Several hundred feet below we could see elephant and Lakes Edward and George joined by the Kazinga Channel. Beyond Lake Edward it was just possible to see the mountains in the Belgian Congo. Further north, the backcloth to this amazing view is formed by the Mountains of the Moon. Alas, only the foothills were visible. David explained that the snow and glaciers on the summits are obscured by heavy rain clouds for most of the year. It was, however, a good chance to see one of the greatest panoramas of the world – and to learn something of the work of the agriculture department staff. They have to work hard to introduce better production practices such as the mulching of the green bananas, and improvement in both the quantity and quality of coffee production.

On another occasion I accompanied Ruffi Darlow, the medical officer, who first came to Uganda in 1946. He has a hospital in Mbarara and several dispensaries out in the rural areas where medical assistants can deal with common complaints. We visited one of these. As we rounded one bend through some lightly wooded country we came upon a group of baboons. Ruffi sprung into action with a whole series of expletives and his shotgun, but they escaped into the bushes. He explained that they can and do attack babies, if left untended whilst their mothers tilled the land. It is the women here who do most of the work in the home and fields; the men are traditionally herders and warriors. He has two nursing sisters on his staff. I met one of them, Jean Hillis, before we set out. She spends quite a lot of her time on tour visiting dispensaries and giving talks on child care and health. She frequently stays alone at rest camps overnight without any fear as to her safety.

I also called on the head of the public works department, Bill Black. His responsibilities extend to the maintenance of the main roads, Protectorate Government buildings and sewage disposal. The township of Mbarara presently has a bucket system and tales abound of people going about their morning duties and being interrupted by the arrival of the bucket emptier who lifts the hatch in the wall behind their seat! I should perhaps make clear at this point that none of the houses or offices have electricity – we await a supply from the Owen Falls Dam; but we do have a water tap at our houses. Additionally, I also had to meet the heads of the education, forestry, veterinary and mines departments. I had a particularly good day out with Jimmy Carolan visiting schools where the application of the children to their work and their seeming pleasure at meeting us were impressive.

On the social side Ann Weir told me that I should call at tea time on the wives of the OC Police, the medical officer and the headmaster of Ntare Secondary School, just outside Mbarara. This is a custom based on the old practice of leaving one's visiting card as a mark of respect on arriving at an administrative headquarters, or station, as up-country townships are often called. None of us have these cards nowadays, but calling is a sensible custom, particularly as each wife gave me tips on recruiting a cook and a houseboy which I shall have to do when I am allocated a house. The wife of the OC Police, known to all as 'Mother', was particularly helpful and has a great reputation for her cooking. Meanwhile, the Ankole Hotel is comfortable enough but I did have trouble the other day with Blanche Hall when I asked for more marmalade at breakfast. "MORE marmalade," she roared. She made me feel like Oliver Twist! She would never have dared to speak to Sir George like that.

The PC expects all his administrative officers to spend a third of their time touring parts of the district and to send him a report on each tour. I am shortly due to join the DC in touring one of Ankole's ten sazas (counties), into which the district is divided. A tour typically lasts ten days and the phrase 'to go on safari' is more commonly used. "Safari is itself a Swahili word of Arabic origin, meaning an expedition and all that pertains to it. It comprises yourself and everybody and everything you take with you – food, tents, rifles, clothing, cooks, servants, escort, porters – but especially porters."[6] Thus it was for Winston Churchill in 1908. It is a little different now. Rifles may be taken if one has a licence to shoot game or, more likely, a shotgun to provide a guinea fowl for the pot. No one is armed in the conventional sense and, I am told, we certainly neither need nor have escorts.

A view of north-west Ankole, taken on the way to Kichwamba.

It seems that our primary purpose on tour is to help in the work and development of the Ankole Local Government and, as I think I mentioned in my letter from Entebbe, there is currently much work involved in implementing a new district administration ordinance. The initial impetus for this had come from the post-war Labour Government. In 1947 the Secretary of State for the Colonies, Arthur Creech Jones, sent a despatch to the governors of all the African territories requiring the development of an efficient and democratic system of local government. (Emphasis was also laid on developing free trade unions and the co-operative movement.) In 1951 CAG Wallis, a British expert, was asked to conduct an enquiry into local government in Uganda and, on the instructions of the DC, I have read his report. It reviewed the development of local government since the native administration ordinance of 1919 and proposed the transfer of substantial powers and responsibilities to local authorities, particularly with regard to the appointment of chiefs and graduated taxation. Wallis envisaged that the assessment of tax would take account of a person's standard of living and/or the valuation of the whole of his possessions. He noted, in the course of his visits to every district, that "there is scarcely any feeling yet among Africans for Uganda as a unified country with a sense of common interest and common purpose."[7] Everyone regarded the Protectorate Government as another name for the British Government and few Africans had any idea of the shape of a future constitution, other than a federation of all the native states and districts, each with its own ruler and ministers. Wallis found that "there is universal distaste for the word 'local', because, for various reasons, the word has lost its derivative meaning and become synonymous with 'inferior' or 'second-class'. They would prefer to be called Native Governments or even to continue to be called Native Administrations. The word 'native' has lost any stigma that it may have acquired in the past and has now been reinstated in its derivative meaning. The word 'African' in the title is also objected to because of a narrow tribal 'nationalism' which seeks to exclude stranger Africans."[8]

Wallis had encountered difficulty in formulating improvements to local government without there being any certainty as to the future constitution of the country. Thus he assumed that Uganda will have a unitary form of government and a democratically elected parliament. He recognised that Buganda will need some form of provincial government. He also recognised the need to take account of the special position of the rulers of Ankole, Bunyoro and Toro. Interestingly, he insisted that British principles of local government be followed as only these "can be imported into Uganda by an administration composed of British officials."[9] But he did recommend that such principles should be adapted to local conditions and his report is full of recommendations, most of which were accepted by the Protectorate Government. The new ordinance is an enabling one and regulations have to be drawn up for application to individual districts. Eric Weir discussed the final draft of the regulations in respect of Ankole with the PC on his recent visit and I was given the task of taking them down to Entebbe, so as not to consign them to the vagaries of the Uganda Post Office. So one afternoon I set off with Bifa, the DC's driver, in a Land Rover for Entebbe. We took it in turns to drive and I found that its short wheelbase produced some uncomfortable shuddering on the murram road. Later models of the Land Rover are now being imported with longer wheelbases and I am told that they are far more comfortable. Not far from Sanga, Bifa pointed excitedly ahead. A lion calmly crossed the road. Was it a man-eater?

Arriving in Kampala I felt really rather superior to the urban lay-abouts as we drove down the main street with 'DC Ankole' painted on the doors in large letters. After all, that meant that I was living in the real Africa, in lion country! I delivered the papers in Entebbe after a night in the Speke Hotel in Kampala. This journey, hardly a safari, should result in Ankole being the first district to be proclaimed under the ordinance.

Next week I am joining Eric Weir on safari for two days at Maseruka, some 30 miles west of Mbarara. I will let you know about that and also a training course which I am due to attend in Entebbe. Luckily, this will coincide with the return from exile of the Kabaka of Buganda.

[1] Speke *Journal of the Discovery of the Nile* 274
[2] Ibid 272
[3] Thomas *The Uganda Journal* Vol 13 No2, 172
[4] Ibid 171
[5] Ibid 172
[6] Churchill *My African Journey* 130
[7] Wallis *Enquiry into African Local Government* 14
[8] Ibid 14
[9] Ibid 15

5: THE KABAKA OF BUGANDA RETURNS IN TRIUMPH

MBARARA
15th November 1955

As an 'exile', admittedly only for a few months so far, I was glad to receive your letter last week. I was not surprised that your Christian sense of fairness led you to question the degree of coercion involved on our side in respect of the various treaties made between the British and the Baganda. We were certainly not guilty of following the example of Stanley, who deployed excessive force in 1875. He killed, on his own wretchedly proud admission, 33 Baganda and injured many more. This was in retaliation for an incident when they had refused to supply him with food, stolen the oars of his boat and pulled his hair! Generally there is no doubt that British explorers acted with restraint, even when provoked. As far as I have been able to find out, fear of other external forces had played a part in the readiness of the Baganda to sign these treaties. They had faced off a much larger force sent in the early 1880s by your distant relative, Colonel Charles Gordon RE, in his role as Governor-General of the Sudan in the service of the Khedive of Egypt. Also the French and Belgians were approaching from the west and the north-west – the Fashoda incident was only two or three years away. This involved a French withdrawal from the West Nile, 500 miles to the south of Khartoum: they had wrongly occupied land in the British sphere of influence. Perhaps, for the Baganda, it was a case of 'better the devil you know'. Speke had earlier made a good impression. We must not forget that Stanley, in spite of his conduct, encouraged the sending of missionaries to Uganda and that Christianity was well received by the people, accompanied as it was by our efforts to end the slave trade.

Leaving history aside, I must now tell you that the last five weeks have been extremely busy and the course at Entebbe, where we met Sir Andrew Cohen, could hardly have been held at a more exciting time, coinciding as it did with the triumphal return of the Kabaka from exile in London.

In mid October I joined the DC on tour in the north of Shema saza, some 20 miles west of Mbarara at Maseruka, where the highlands of north-west Ankole begin to rise sharply to 7,000 feet. I think I told you in my last letter that there are ten sazas in the district, each under the control of a saza chief. Each saza is itself divided into about seven or eight gombololas, each in the charge of a gombolola chief. It was raining when I arrived at the gombolola headquarters, October being one of our wettest months, having an average rainfall of six inches. The water was cascading off the corrugated-iron roof, some elementary gutters having fallen to the ground. I found the DC sitting at a table made of hand-hewn planks on a dais at one end of the meeting hall. The table was piled with registers, tax tickets, both for the flat-rate Protectorate Government poll tax and local taxes; also market fee tickets and some cash. With the DC were the gombolola chief and his clerk, wearing anxious frowns. As I walked in Eric was calling for the records of the tax tickets supplied by the saza chief's office and for the receipts issued by that office. He was checking all these against the tax registers, tickets and cash. An apparent discrepancy was found and Eric wrestled with this, before discovering a mistake in the addition of one column of figures. I was surprised at the thoroughness of this audit which seemed to take quite a long time, but the DC rightly believes in setting high standards of accuracy and rectitude in financial matters.

Next the DC turned to the local court records and his interpreter, when necessary, recounted the charges made against individuals and punishments awarded. These mostly related to a person's failure to comply with local government bye-laws. Two of these require householders to maintain famine reserves and to build proper latrines, major adjuncts of a safer and healthier society. The former have to be raised up from the ground in small thatched granaries and the latter have to be dug down some ten feet deep and to be topped by a concrete slab in the French style. Another bye-law forbids drinking in the day time! There were no appeals to the DC recorded in these cases; appeals tend to be more common in civil cases which often arise from boundary disputes with neighbours.

Once he was satisfied with all the financial and legal records, the DC consulted his tour book for the saza and, with the advice of the gombolola chief, selected one of the mulukas for inspection that afternoon. I had better explain muluka (parish). Just as a saza is divided into gombololas so each gombolola is divided into some seven or eight mulukas, each with a muluka chief in charge. This is the hierarchical pattern of government which the early administrators found when they arrived in Buganda and which they extended to most of the rest of the country. The tour book contains reports of all inspections by the DC or one of his assistants over the years. The totals of taxes collected and cases judged are recorded. The progress, or lack of it, in introducing measures to improve housing, agricultural production and any problems being encountered by departmental officers are also noted. The dates of visits to the different mulukas are listed and Eric was thus able to choose an area which had not been visited for about two and a half years. After a lunch of sandwiches we drove to the chosen muluka. The gombolola chief had sent a local government askari, kitted out in a khaki uniform and a red fez, to advise the muluka chief of the DC's intention. These askaris are local police and messengers and their powers are limited to the enforcement of all the local government bye-laws. They have no powers under the laws of Uganda.

The muluka chief greeted us warmly. Deliberately he had not been given much time to alert his people to the visit as the DC wanted to see things as they are, not after they had been whitewashed! After Eric decided on a particular route we all set off on foot. We stopped at every household where we were greeted by its members. It was clear that most were making good progress; windows had been installed in most of their houses, crops, especially coffee, were well mulched. I found it fascinating to be invited into their homes for the first time. Most had raised wooden platforms for sleeping, and pots and pans were placed on small wooden racks. Often a fire smouldered at the centre and, as the smoke was left to find its own way up through the thatch, the whole interior was rather blackened and smelt, not unpleasantly, of ash and soot. Women generally knelt on the floor and greeted me in soft tones. At the larger homesteads, corrugated-iron roofs helped to collect rainwater, a major advance from total dependence on the daily collection of water in drums from the nearest stream or bore-hole. At one of these we met one of the Geological Survey drillers, Cyril Whyatt. He is seconded to the local government and that day he was repairing the hand-pumping mechanism. However, most of his time he is busy drilling new bore-holes; the department started its drilling programme in 1931.

On we went. The path was mainly indistinct; it wound amongst the green bananas, along the edge of plots of coffee, through scrubby woodland and down beside an extensive swamp. It was strange to find this at 5,000 feet. The river Koga drains the swamp towards the Ruizi river which flows eastwards just south of Mbarara. (No doubt the science of geomorphology – remember how we both decided not to pursue that subject at Cambridge – will be applied eventually to explain the physical features of Ankole.) People materialised from nowhere and we soon gathered quite a following. We examined famine reserves and pit latrines. The muluka chief opened the top of a granary, demonstrating that the required amount of grain was present. This depends on the number of people in the household. He also checked that the millet was fresh. We probably only covered about half the area of the muluka, but the visit must have reinforced the authority of this chief. The DC congratulated him at the end of the walk and he proudly produced a visitors book for our signatures. We returned to the rest camp by Land Rover and Ann Weir greeted us. I had not realised that she was also on tour; she had spent some of the day at a school and had talked to some of the mothers about the care of their children.

The next morning the DC held a lukiiko, which in this context means a meeting for the people at the gombolola headquarters. It may also mean a meeting of local government councillors. All the muluka chiefs were present, together with an assistant agricultural officer and the medical assistant from the nearby dispensary. Before the proceedings began the DC made a point of speaking to the departmental officers to hear whether they had any points which he could emphasise on their behalf. There were benches for them and for the chiefs but most of the hundred or so local men sat on the floor of the large council hall. A few women came and observed the proceedings cautiously through the open windows. After a friendly greeting by the gombolola chief, Eric spoke through his interpreter for about 20 minutes or so. Although he knows some Runyankore he could not easily explain current Protectorate Government policies in the local language; particularly in regard to the greater powers which will shortly be given to the Ankole Local Government.

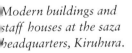

Modern buildings and staff houses at the saza headquarters, Kiruhura.

He stressed the fact that the governments could only provide more and better schools, roads, dispensaries and houses for Ankole Local Government staff if the people increased their wealth by planting more coffee. He then went on to say that with more money they would all be able to pay higher taxes! Needless to say this failed to produce any applause. But it is precisely this equation which has led to Uganda's current development and increasing prosperity. At the request of the gombolola chief he called for a better response to the muluka chiefs' arrangements for communal work. This work, known as 'bulungi bwansi', meaning 'for the good of the country', enables local tracks and school buildings to be improved by voluntary labour. Finally the DC gave plenty of time for questions. These included demands for higher prices for coffee, more teachers and more medicines in the dispensary. The complaint about the coffee price has some legitimacy, as the Protectorate Government operates a price assistance fund, withholding some of the price payable to growers when world prices are high, in order to inflate the return to growers when prices fall. The farmers regard this as a form of taxation. Although some complained about the taxes the atmosphere was generally very good-hearted and occasionally humorous. At the end one or two older men left muttering moodily. After all, no one likes talk of higher taxes, in Uganda or at home!

I returned to Mbarara the next day in order to prepare for the journey to Entebbe. As I left him, the DC said that I should spend a few days with Russel Barty on tour when I come back from the course. After that he intimated that I should then be ready to go out on my own, initially just to check the books and tour the villages, rather than to hold meetings at which I might not be able to answer some of the questions.

When I arrived at the Nsamizi Training Centre in Entebbe, I quickly learned that my five colleagues had also been 'on safari pupilari'. A number of newly appointed departmental officers, some of whom had been on the *Kenya Castle*, were also attending the three-week course. Under the leadership of the director of training, Pip Coutts, we were given a series of briefings by the heads of the various departments. We visited missions, research centres, schools and a housing estate; plus a nearby slum. We also had further Luganda lessons and we all passed a written and oral examination. This may not be of much value at present but, who knows, some of us may be posted to Buganda one day.

Our first working day, Monday 17th October, coincided with the Kabaka of Buganda's return from exile and the day inevitably became a public holiday on a grand scale. His Highness landed at Entebbe airport at 9.00am and he was met by Sir Andrew Cohen, who had withdrawn recognition from him and deported him to London in November 1953. There had been a precedent for the deportation of a Kabaka but before I tell you about that and the events leading up to Mutesa II's exile and return, I should explain more fully how Buganda became such a significant part of Uganda. Here's where that list of dates might come in useful.

Before the early explorers arrived in the area which is now Uganda it was occupied by rival rulers and warring tribes. The principal protagonists were the Baganda and the Banyoro. The easiest route to this area lay through

Egypt and the Sudan but the Mahdi's rebellion in 1883 largely inhibited its use by Europeans. Thus the early explorers, missionaries and Arab traders were generally forced to approach Uganda from the south or east. Buganda, already well organised and a richly fertile country, was therefore always at the centre of new events, not least the introduction of education by the missionaries. After Kabaka Mutesa I died in 1884, Buganda lost its ascendancy over Bunyoro, largely because Kabaka Mwanga was less able than his predecessor. Discontent in Buganda led to civil war. There was confusion and conflict until Lugard, in the service of the Imperial British East Africa Company, defeated the Mukama of Bunyoro, Kabalega, and forced a settlement on the warring parties in Buganda in 1890. After Portal had recommended that Uganda should be made a Protectorate, the British Government soon found that his estimate of £20,000 a year for the costs of governing Uganda had risen to £300,000! This was mainly due to the expense of dealing with a mutiny of Sudanese troops and keeping the peace between the adherents of the Protestant and Catholic missions. Worse, Mwanga and Kabalega rebelled in 1897 and were finally apprehended in 1899 by Colonel Trevor Ternan, the acting Commissioner. Both were deported to Kisumu in what is now Kenya and eventually to the Seychelles.

The British Government at the time of that first deportation was determined to clarify its policy towards Buganda. Lord Salisbury appointed Sir Harry Johnston as Special Commissioner in 1899. He made a new Agreement in 1900 with the three Regents, Mwanga's successor being the young Kabaka Daudi Chwa. It was called the Uganda Agreement but its wording clearly indicated that Buganda was one of a number of provinces in the Uganda Protectorate. Sir Harry could not have known that Article 6 would become a major source of contention:

> So long as the Kabaka, chiefs, and people of Uganda shall
> conform to the laws and regulations instituted for their
> governance by Her Majesty's Government, and shall co-
> operate loyally with Her Majesty's Government in the
> organisation and administration of the said Kingdom of
> Uganda, Her Majesty's Government agrees to recognise
> the Kabaka of Uganda as the native ruler of the province
> of Uganda under Her Majesty's protection and over-rule.

This Article was not a problem for many years. When Sir Andrew Cohen was appointed Governor in 1952 he brought with him from the Colonial Office a determination to speed up political advance. Unusually, he had not served abroad before. By 1953 he had already agreed with the Kabaka that the number of elected members in the Buganda Lukiiko (parliament) should be increased to 60, albeit they might be elected indirectly through electoral colleges. At the same time a number of departmental services were due to be handed over to the Buganda Government in the context of the Wallis Report. A further 12 representative members were to be nominated to the Protectorate's Legislative Council bringing the total to 28, of whom 14 were to be Africans. Of these, four would represent Buganda. There were other advances which involved the transfer of more influence and power from the Kabaka to his ministers and to the Lukiiko. An announcement of these changes, all of which had been agreed with the Kabaka, concluded that the Uganda Protectorate had been, and would continue to be, developed as a unitary state. Also the Kingdom of Buganda would continue to go forward under the government of His Highness the Kabaka and play its part, as a province and a component part of the Protectorate.

Unfortunately, these plans were not uppermost in the mind of the Secretary of State, Oliver Lyttleton, when he made a passing reference to the possibility of a Federation of the East African Territories, in a speech on 30th June 1953. The prospect that the Baganda might come under the control of the Kenya settlers was sufficient to cause the Kabaka to question his earlier agreement with Sir Andrew's political reforms. The Kabaka demanded independence for Buganda on its own and that the Foreign Office, rather than the Colonial Office, should handle his country's relations with Britain. Great efforts were made to reassure the Kabaka that the Secretary of State's speech, which was said to be informal, posed no threat to Buganda. In their eyes no such speech could ever be regarded as informal. By November 1953 there was complete deadlock and the Kabaka refused to withdraw his demands. After a visit by the Governor to London, plans were made to remove the Kabaka. His Highness maintained his intransigence at a final meeting with the Governor at Government House on 30th November. He was certainly not co-operating loyally with Her Majesty's Government and Sir Andrew signed a deportation order. Within a very short time the Kabaka and Robert Ntambi, his Aide-de-Camp, were aboard an RAF Hastings which had landed at Entebbe, ostensibly with engine problems. As soon as they were seated the Kabaka and his Aide handed over their hand guns and were each given toothbrushes and other essentials. The RAF flew them to London and they went by taxi to the Savoy Hotel.

Meanwhile in Buganda there was very little civil unrest; the police had been well deployed. The Governor emphasised that this action was not an attack on the kabakaship and that the election of a new Kabaka would be welcomed, under the terms of the 1900 Agreement. There was some support for this amongst some influential Baganda, for Mutesa II had not been universally popular. But, notwithstanding an announcement by the Secretary of State in the House of Commons that the decision to deport the Kabaka was final, it proved increasingly difficult for the Protectorate Government to govern Buganda in the absence of His Highness. The deportation damaged the pride of the Baganda in their kingdom to an extent that normal relations between Protectorate Government officials and the Baganda deteriorated rapidly. A political party, the Uganda National Congress, began to win support in Buganda for the first time.

The Lukiiko sent a delegation to the Secretary of State in London and, as so often happens in government, a committee was formed in February 1954 under the chairmanship of Sir Keith Hancock, Professor of British Commonwealth Affairs in the University of London, to consider the constitutional problems in Buganda. The Lukiiko's nominees to this committee included some of the best educated and 'neutral' Baganda, that is, those who were neither political agitators nor died-in-the-wool traditionalists. The Governor took a prominent role in many months of negotiations. During this time the legality of the Protectorate Government's deportation of the Kabaka was tested in the courts, and eventually a compromise was achieved which permitted the return of the Kabaka. To some extent this outcome was helped when the Chief Justice, His Honour Sir John Griffin, ruled that the deportation was not justified under Article 6 of the 1900 Agreement, although it could be justified under Article 20. The difference lay in the use of 'Kabaka, chiefs and people' in Article 6 and the use of 'Kabaka, chiefs or people' in Article 20. Such are the niceties of constitutional law. A new transitional agreement was drawn up and signed by the Governor and three personal representatives of the Kabaka on 15th August, whilst we were still at sea off Cape Guardafui. Thus the way was paved for the return of His Highness.

This we witnessed when standing by the road to Entebbe airport just below Government House. The route was marked every now and then by great arches of welcome constructed of elephant grass and decorated with shields and spears. Throngs of very excited Baganda packed every inch of the roadside. The Kabaka stood in a large open limousine, the first of three Rolls Royces. Some two or three hundred cars followed, bearing the welcoming party which had gathered at the airport soon after dawn. The day passed peacefully although some of my colleagues were mildly heckled later. The welcome festivities, including the formal signing of the 1955 Agreement, continued for some days. There was a regatta on the lake shore and a garden party at Government House to which we were invited.

The gardens are extensive but hardly large enough for the thousands of people who gathered on the lawns for tea and cakes. When the Governor escorted His Highness amongst the people the crowd forced me back against a low wall of knee height which marks the edge of the main lawn and a considerable drop to further gardens below. I thought at one point that my knees would buckle and that I would disappear backwards. As the Kabaka approached I found that everyone around me was going down on their knees and I wondered for a moment what to do! I remained upright, just, as the kneeling Baganda forced me back even more tightly against the low wall. I had a very good view of the slight and immaculate Captain of the Grenadier Guards. Sir Andrew was heard by one of my colleagues muttering to the Kabaka, "Let's get back"; presumably to the wide, cool veranda which runs the length of GH on the garden side.

The lower gardens of Government House beyond the wall.

Two days later I was able to enjoy the garden and the pool more exclusively. Edward Cunningham knows Charles Lewis, who is Aide-de-Camp to Sir Andrew. Charles invited Edward, David Pasteur, Robin Palmer and me to have a swim at the end of a long day of lectures at Nsamizi. We all changed in Charles' room and made our way, in our swimming trunks, down the back stairs and then through the elegant panelled dining room. There the long table, laid with fine china and silver, was surrounded with red leather chairs bearing the EIIR monogram. We only began to feel more comfortable as we crossed the veranda and the lawns towards the pool. This is situated to one side of some beautiful rose beds above which the high flagpole was flying the Governor's standard. Lady Cohen was nearby and watched as we all dived in. I don't normally dive; I never mastered that skill. But these surroundings seemed to encourage some fast learning, so I followed the others and inevitably belly-flopped!

Later, changed but not very smart, we were asked by Lady Cohen to stay for a drink and were briefly joined by Sir Andrew. He had to leave us to greet Sir Godfrey Huggins, the Prime Minister of the Federation of Rhodesia and Nyasaland, whose aeroplane was being refuelled at Entebbe. They strode across the lawns deep in conversation for about half an hour. We all hoped that the Baganda would remain oblivious to Sir Godfrey's visit in view of their antipathy to federalism. As long ago as 1927 the then Kabaka feared that a move to provide some common services throughout East Africa might result in the diminishing of Buganda's importance. It is not surprising therefore that Oliver Lyttleton's remarks in 1953 caused so much disturbance in Buganda. But common services were necessarily developed during the war and the East African High Commission now successfully co-ordinates the railways and harbours, posts and telegraphs, income tax, customs and excise, research and statistics, and civil aviation.

Amidst all the celebrations of the Kabaka's return there was new hope that the latest Agreement will settle the issue of Buganda's role in a unified Uganda. But I came across evidence that this might not be so. In addition to our invitations to Government House, we have severally been invited to tea or dinner during our course by senior officials. Some of us were asked to tea by Betty Boyd, the wife of Lachlan Boyd, the Minister of Local Government. She presided over a range of silver teapots, sandwiches and cakes on the veranda of their lovely house and we were offered the choice of Indian or China tea. Later the Minister returned and it was clear from his remarks to his wife that the new Agreement was already under some strain. Apparently the Katikiro, the Prime Minister of Buganda, had made some statement that at the least breached the spirit of the new accord.

As our course came to an end Pip Coutts and his wife Alison invited Sir Andrew and Lady Cohen to their house one evening and we were all given an informal opportunity to ask questions. We had heard of Sir Andrew's reputation; he had achieved a double first in classics, became an under-secretary in Whitehall in his 30s and was well known as a man of enormous energy and temper! But we found him relaxed and informative and fully prepared to spend more than an hour and a half with us. He seemed quite reluctant to leave until he was sure that we had run out of questions. The possibility of an East African federation was raised and pronounced 'out of the question'. He did not see it as a corollary of economic co-operation which he was keen to promote. He talked of his plans for the Uganda Development Corporation, the co-operative movement and the national parks. He considered that Buganda must inevitably be in the lead in political development but did not think that federation between the different parts of Uganda was practical, due to the inequalities of the various provinces and districts. By the end of the evening he had demonstrated his dynamism and it was quite clear that his dispute with the Kabaka arose because the latter had come between him and his plans for rapid political advance. His Excellency finally wished us well and it is likely that we shall all meet him again, as his energy takes him on frequent and lengthy tours to the furthest corners of the country.

The next day I collected my car, a Standard Vanguard pick-up. I was very excited because I had never owned a car before. It is not really mine as I bought it with a government loan. I can only afford that on the assumption that my mileage allowances will be sufficient to meet the repayments. So I drove westwards, counting the miles, alone on an African journey for the first time. When I sighted Mbarara in the distance, its white shops in the middle of that lovely stretch of hill-ringed plain, I noticed that the sun cast deep shadows in the bush-filled valleys which etched the sides of the grassy hills. I felt as though I was returning home, such had been my initial welcome in Ankole. And what an interesting three weeks it had been. It is very surprising that a governor should take so much time and trouble to talk to a bunch of raw, newly-arrived district officers. Sir Andrew and his wife could not have been more approachable nor more forthcoming.

6: THE MURDER OF HARRY ST GEORGE GALT

BIHANGA
10th February 1956

After I returned from Entebbe, I accompanied Russel Barty on part of his tour in the south-west of Ankole near the border with Kigezi District as the DC had suggested. This is a very mountainous and over-populated area where great care has to be taken to prevent soil erosion on the steep hillsides which rise to over 10,000 feet. I visited the area last month, staying at the White Horse Inn at Kabale, the district headquarters. There I met a new ADC, Nick Bateman-Champain, who arrived last December. Exceptionally, he had not attended a 'Devonshire' course as the Colonial Office was anxious to increase our numbers in the shortest possible time.

In response to your letter in which you asked if I was still at Blanche Hall's mercy, I am delighted to tell you that I escaped earlier than expected as Brian Watson, the forestry officer, asked me to share his large bungalow with him. The forest department is responsible for some seven percent of the land area. Three weeks ago I was allocated my own quarters, a small old bungalow with a pleasant veranda. My immediate neighbours are Mike Ball, a police officer, and Roy and Margaret Seal; he is a geologist. We all have a delightful view of the hills to the south. Immediately below my bungalow there are some new houses. Freddie Sheridan and his wife 'Puss' live in one. I think I told you he is ADC II and I accompanied him on a tour near the Kagera river, our boundary with Tanganyika in the south. There I met 'Beetle', Jack and their sister, 'Spadge' Collins. They are the only British 'settlers' in Ankole, excluding missionaries, and have mining concessions for tin and beryl. (They are not really settlers because they have to renew their resident status at regular intervals.) They entertained us most royally to dinner at their camp. Every Easter they host a cricket match at Mbarara and they bring in enough supplies of food and drink to entertain everyone, including some of the Asian shopkeepers who enjoy cricket.

Now, for the first time, I am touring on my own in Mitoma saza, a hilly area in the north of Ankole where the land lies mainly between 4,500 and 6,000 feet. It is 30 miles from Mbarara and close to the border with Toro District. I am not really alone as I am accompanied by an interpreter, an office messenger, a driver for the Land Rover and Joseph my cook. We usually begin our tours on a Monday so we travel out to a saza on the Sunday afternoon. After a farewell drink in the club before lunch, I headed due north in my brand new Vanguard across the flat anthill-strewn grassy plains of Kashari saza. The murram road is well constructed and is equipped with signposts at the few junctions that exist. After an hour or so, the hills of Buhweju saza came into sight to the north-west. This was once an independent kingdom but it is now depopulated due to its remoteness. I was glad to see that the high land continued eastwards towards Mitoma and the road began to twist and turn through a more exciting stretch of country amongst the foothills of Singiro, the highest peak in Ankole, 7,126 feet. I noted that the summit would be an excellent place from which to observe the homesteads and crops of at least two of the gombololas of Mitoma. I wondered if the chiefs would be able and willing to come with me and noted a possible route up to the summit. I drove on to my destination, Ibanda, the saza headquarters. This comprises a small Asian trading centre and a few African shops, the saza chief's office and house, a dispensary, a gaol and, nearby, a large Roman Catholic Mission. I was pleased to find that the rest house was set on a steep hillside with southerly views in the direction of Mbarara. Needless to say there was no telephone. It was a strange feeling to be so far from the 'civilisation' of Mbarara but I hoped that the courses at Oxford and Entebbe, together with the experience of going on tour with the DC and his two senior assistants, would be sufficient unto the day. That is until four days ago, when I thought that I might become the second administrative officer to be assassinated in Uganda.

There are usually structures like this at rest houses, so that our tents do not have to withstand the force of heavy rains.

My tent was soon pitched in the compound under a low-walled thatched structure, open at one end. Then the saza chief, the Sekibobo of Mitoma, arrived. He is a man of some 50 years and his experience in the work of

On the veranda of the rest house at Ibanda with Tosca, my new black labrador, with a white patch from the White Fathers' mission near Mbarara.

running the local government obviously gives him enjoyment. As we drank tea on the veranda of the rest house, he explained the main problems facing the saza. A concern is the resettlement of some farmers from Kigezi. Here less than a tenth of the ground is cultivated and, with the agreement of the Ankole Local Government and the people, they are brought in by the lorry load, voluntarily, and given fertile land. The scheme benefits Ankole as an increase in the area of land under cultivation acts as a barrier against the incursion of the tsetse fly which is endemic in Toro. The Sekibobo also told me that there is some tension between the Banyankole and Batoro, the people of the Kingdom of Toro. Violent crime is at an unusually high level compared to the rest of the district.

While Joseph prepared my supper, I set off westwards along the dusty road that leads towards the Toro boundary, in the general direction of Lake George and the Mountains of the Moon. I am told that these can be seen quite often from the hills around here as they are only some 40 miles away. After about two miles I came to the stone-built Galt memorial, a white-painted cone some 15 feet high. It was built to commemorate the death of Harry St George Galt on 19th May 1905 at the site of an earlier rest house. He is the only administrative officer murdered in the relatively short history of our rule in Uganda. I had not expected to find his memorial, although I already knew of his death through working in the Galt Memorial Hall in Mbarara. (This is used as the magistrate's court, near the district commissioner's office. As a third-class magistrate I have been learning how to conduct preliminary hearings into cases in which an accused person faces a charge of murder. A preliminary inquiry is necessary in order to record statements of the accused and of the witnesses whilst memories are fresh, the actual trial before a judge being usually some months later.) But I was not particularly perturbed as I returned from the memorial to the rest house; after all Galt had been murdered 50 years ago; no other administrative officer has ever been harmed.

After a good supper I read the tour book before I retired to my tent. In the next two days I visited three of the gombololas and routinely but rigorously examined all the financial records. It was quite clear that the chiefs and the clerks were operating efficiently. I turned to the court records. In criminal cases the evidence is usually fairly straightforward as the offences arise from breaches of the bye-laws. Failure to pay taxes, trading without a licence, having insufficient famine reserves were the recurrent themes in the court registers. I quickly became familiar with the Runyankore records. On the second day one exceptional case required translation. I was told that it involved 'having carnal knowledge of a goat'.

My sheltered background left me in some mystery about that until my interpreter gave me a more explicit translation! As elsewhere civil cases mostly arise from land disputes and there were plenty of these, a reflection of the tensions on the border with Toro.

This book work occupied most of each morning and in the afternoons I walked or cycled around a muluka as much as possible. Cycling on a borrowed bicycle has its limitations because the paths are of a variable quality and often just a walk-way through banana shambas, a widely used Kiswahili name for cultivated areas. (The Kiswahili language is commonly spoken throughout Kenya and Tanganyika. It is understood by many in Uganda, but the Baganda resist its use, associating it with British settlement in Kenya and with the Arab slave traders.) The bananas are mainly the green variety, known as matoke; when steamed they provide more than half the people's food supplies. Every now and then we came across a farmer with four or five huge bunches of matoke precariously balanced on the back of a bicycle. (The bicycle is a form of transport for almost anything; large bedsteads are commonly balanced on the rear carrier.) Great emphasis is based by the agricultural staff on mulching in order to conserve water in the soil and to restrict the growth of weeds. The mulch is mainly provided by pruning the branches and leaves of the banana trees. The local agricultural assistant accompanied the muluka chief and me. Occasionally the Sekibobo came himself but he was confident enough in his chiefs, and maybe in me, to leave us alone. The agricultural assistant was keen to demonstrate his success in helping the people raise their standards of cultivation and thus their income and wealth. In parts of Mitoma it is possible to grow arabica coffee and the farmers are encouraged to plant as many bushes as possible, but then there is the work of harvesting and drying and achieving a high quality product. Not all the people are keen, once their basic requirements have been met, to work quite as hard as the agricultural assistant suggests. Once the essentials of a corrugated-iron roof, school fees, a radio, a bicycle and sometimes water tanks have been purchased, there is an understandable tendency for some, in the heat of the day, to conserve energy. The farmers no doubt find it hard to appreciate exactly why the Protectorate Government pays them less than the world price when it is high and promises to support the price they receive when the market declines. After all most of them will not have travelled beyond Mbarara, unless they fought with The King's African Rifles in the last war. Yet much has been achieved. At Entebbe I learnt that the value of Uganda's coffee exports have risen from about £23,000 in 1914 to £20 million last year.

On the afternoon of the second day I went to Lukiri in the extreme south-west of the saza to visit a remote gombolola. Using the Land Rover we were able to drive some way towards a hill known as Kabuchenge, which is 5,000 feet high. With the gombolola chief, muluka chief and agricultural assistant, I walked some way over the splendid grassy uplands. There were good vantage points from which to see the houses and cultivation in the valleys below us. I am not entirely sure that my colleagues enjoyed this exercise as much as I did. I made a mental note to make the ascent of Singiro by myself at the weekend.

The local chiefs inspect a farmer's famine reserve in a granary.

I greatly enjoyed contact with the people and sought to encourage and cajole them as necessary. The farmers were generally very keen to show me around their shambas and, of course, I checked the famine reserves. These are essential in order to lessen the risk of hunger following crop failures and each family is required by the local government to maintain a reserve. Everyone seemed very friendly, and I was invited into some of the larger houses and asked to sign the visitors book. This is one of a number of British customs which have been widely adopted. Others are group photographs, in which the people tend to strike attitudes in the manner of the Victorians, and association football. (Most districts have enough 'mad' expatriates to raise a XV for the other variety.)

But the keenness of some of the farmers was as nothing compared to that of the children in the schools. It would have been quite impossible to have passed by without spending some time in the classrooms. I was struck by the diligence and dedication of the teachers. They work in open-sided buildings with little furniture and equipment but with visible success. Invariably there is time for a song, in English, a display of football on a bare patch of ground, or even a parade before the ADC! There is occasional friction between the young educated teachers and the local chiefs, but generally the latter support the schools and organise the people who carry out bulungi bwansi. This includes improvement of school buildings, the hunting of wild boars which damage crops, and the maintenance of tracks and paths. All these tasks require combined muscle power.

All continued to go well as I toured the county each day. Most evenings the Sekibobo came to see me at the rest house for a glass of beer and to talk about my day's experience. One evening we had hardly sat down on the veranda, with its glorious views over the plains to the south and the hills of Buhweju, when a messenger arrived with cries of anguish. He told us that there had been a murder near the Roman Catholic Mission at Kyakagongo, two miles beyond the Galt memorial. We drove there at once, passing the memorial, and found a crowd wailing and lamenting around one of the huts. We were told that a woman had been stabbed to death inside and that two others were missing. I was invited into the hut, but I shirked viewing the body; if I had, my subsequent anxiety might have been even worse. Messengers were despatched to summon police help from Mbarara, using an emergency system of runners, the gombolola askaris. The Sekibobo ordered the local chiefs to begin to take statements from the villagers and to search the hill above the village. This soon proved impracticable and, as the evening light faded, we returned to Ibanda leaving an askari to guard the scene. I can assure you that I did not enjoy the supper Joseph had cooked for me. When Galt was assassinated on the veranda of the first rest house, he "called for his cook and said, 'Look, cook, a savage has speared me'; and thereupon he fell down dead!"[1] I did not enjoy the night. Nothing in the 'Devonshire' course prepared me for this situation, nor guided my thoughts away from the possibility that the murderer, or maybe a gang of murderers, might decide to repeat past history. I did not sleep at all. I passed some of the night sitting on the veranda of the rest house, which somehow seemed more secure than the recesses of the tent shelter: at least I could see an attacker coming! I was indeed very frightened, as you may surmise. (The assassin's motive is by no means clear, it may possibly have arisen from rivalry between chiefs in Toro and Ankole.)

Dawn came – none could have been more welcome – and with it some news. The bodies of the two missing women had been found on the hillside above their village. This triple murder clearly horrified all the local people. The Sekibobo and I decided that there was little that we could do. We agreed to keep to my programme of visits, as the Uganda police would arrive shortly from Mbarara. Somewhat to the unease of the local chiefs, I asked to climb the hills beyond the scene of the murder and near the Toro boundary. Here we had excellent views of the plots of coffee in the valleys. The hills are not unlike those of mid-Wales, rounded slopes covered with long grass. Suddenly we came upon a view of Lake George and the lower slopes of the Ruwenzori. The chiefs, an askari and my Land Rover driver could not understand my excitement as I lined them up for a photograph. The snow and glaciers were unfortunately hidden behind the clouds which almost always cover the range. Its highest peak is Margherita, 16,763 feet. That evening, on our return to the rest camp we met Mike Ball, the inspector of police whom I mentioned earlier. He had brought several Uganda policemen and you may guess that I was greatly relieved at their presence.

A local chief found this campsite. The tent is shaded by two acacia trees.

I was due, in any event, to move camp the next day to the eastern end of Mitoma, and I have spent the weekend here near Bihanga. There is no rest camp, but the local chief has found an excellent site for my tent beneath two acacia trees. Successive generations of district commissioners have sited rest camps so that they have the best possible views, and now the chiefs have certainly learned how to choose a good spot for a tent. As I write I am enjoying the evening view of the plains of north Ankole, the home of the long-horned Ankole cattle.

On Sunday I climbed Singiro with a local village chief who volunteered to come with me. We made the 2,000 foot ascent with no difficulty in spite of the absence of paths. The views from the summit at 7,126 feet ranged across a large part of north Ankole but the Ruwenzori range 40 miles away was, yet again, shrouded in cloud. However, I enjoyed the ascent and we made our way back to the village of Lweshe. None of the villagers, as far as I could make out, had ever been on the summit. I suspect that my guide had not been there before either, but he certainly knew the way through the dense scrub on the lower slopes. He was pleased with the bottles of beer I gave him, but no doubt wondered why I could not simply rest in my camp at the weekend, instead of climbing in the midday sun. This was not just recreation; I had a very good view of the farming and housing improvements across a large part of the saza. The number of new houses with corrugated-iron roofs is now quite considerable. They glisten in the sunlight like stars among the banana shambas!

I also visited the new extension of the railway from Kampala to Kasese. The Sekibobo and I walked along some of the track and admired the cuttings and embankments. The line is due to be opened in November and its construction is a major achievement. He told me that the line makes a complete loop as it descends the escarpment to the north of Lake George. It will carry copper from the new Kilembe mines in the foothills of the Ruwenzori to Jinja, where a smelter is due to begin operation next year. It is estimated that £1.5 million worth of ingots will be sent in the first year to Mombasa and thence to the world's markets. A lesser achievement, but one eagerly awaited here, is the construction of an access road to Bihanga station. This will enable the despatch of cattle to the markets at Kampala. The contractor is Basil Yourtaglou, a Greek adventurer who has useful skills and commands the respect of his 'labours', his term for the local people who dig the channels for the culverts. He uses a small bulldozer to cut a level swathe through the bush. One of my tasks has been to inspect his progress using some elementary knowledge of road-building gained on the course at Oxford. The crucial requirement is to match the provision and capacity of the culverts to the greatest likely flow of water in the valleys – for me more a matter of hypothesis than mathematical calculation!

This is at present a very remote corner of Uganda but the railway will bring change. Today some young children fled before me in terror. I was worried until the Sekibobo explained that they had not seen a white man before. Maybe I was walking where no white man had ever walked? I had a feeling of pioneering, that is until I climbed back into the Land Rover which can of course go almost anywhere. We returned to the rest camp at Ibanda to hear reassuring news: a messenger had arrived to report that three men have been arrested for the murders and are being held in the local gaol.

I shall return to Mbarara tomorrow and the deepest impression I have is the respect which has been given to me by these extremely poor, yet so very cheerful people. The key to this seems to lie in the fact that any district officer on tour is regarded and addressed as 'Bwana DC', which means, 'District Commissioner, Sir'. Yet all the chiefs and most of the people know that I am not Eric Weir. As our touring uniform is a khaki jacket and shorts, everyone can see that my knees are very white and new to the country! Respect, yes, but there is no trace of subservience and we must owe much to our predecessors at the end of the last century. Lugard, for one, set high standards. "Gordon says that an Administrator in Africa should be one-third soldier and two-thirds civilian. No country in the world demands a more careful selection of the men who are to control it, for in no other are they so isolated. According to their first impressions of the white man, so will the natives form the estimate of our character and our methods. A great responsibility thus rests on the first pioneers. The respect they claim as their due, the deference accorded to them, the trust in their courage and their justice are heirlooms to their successors. But if they should fail to establish the character of the white man on a basis superior to any the savage has yet known, it will take long to eradicate the impression and to re-establish our ascendancy. I would far sooner place a good reliable native in a position of responsibility than a weak or vicious European."[2] Lugard was certainly not an advocate of innate white superiority. His final sentence makes this clear. His emphasis was on leadership, justice and setting an example of good character.

All this means that I have an impossible act to follow. You will no doubt meet those at home who think that we rule by force. Certainly force has had to be used occasionally, for example at the time of the 1945 riots in Buganda when the Protectorate Government sought to acquire more land for Makerere College. This was misrepresented by some as a prelude to the introduction of European plantations! More relevant to me, as I shivered through the night following the murders, was the stern reaction that followed the assassination of Galt. There was a lengthy enquiry by George Wilson, then the Deputy Commissioner of Uganda. Two junior Ankole chiefs, Gabrieli Rwakakaiga and Isaka Nyakayaga, were accused of culpable negligence and indifference because they failed to report certain facts which would have led to the arrest of the assassin, Rutaraka. He committed suicide. The two chiefs were later found guilty by the High Court at Entebbe of having abetted murder. They appealed to the Court of Appeal for East Africa at Mombasa and were released, but the Commissioner, Sir Hesketh Bell, considered that it was necessary for the peace and good order of the country that the two should nevertheless be punished for their negligence: they were exiled to the coast.

"It was felt that this was not sufficient and that the heinousness of killing a British official must be brought home vividly to the whole population of Ankole, and I decided to adopt a form of collective punishment. Cattle being the principal wealth of the country, I therefore imposed a fine of 1,000 head on the King – Kahaya – and 200 on each of the principal Chiefs of the country. The male peasantry had to work for a month on the making of new roads, while a special tax was levied to pay for the erection of a Memorial Hall at the capital, Mbarara, in memory of Galt. These proceedings may appear high-handed and arbitrary, but it must be remembered that we were dealing with the people of a country in its earliest stages. It was essential to impress upon the natives throughout the Protectorate the sanctity of the lives of our small staff of officers, and the lesson that was given to the people of Ankole was so striking that it is unlikely that it will ever have to be repeated."[3]

Roy Seal and Gil Baird enjoy an early evening game of golf, with the Galt Memorial Hall in the background.

Time has proved his point as my colleagues and I go about the country unarmed. Though vulnerable, we are not under any threat and therefore there is no risk. My anxiety was unfounded.

I really must draw this letter to a close as the Tilley light in my tent is about to go out, and I shall have to leave early in the morning to finish the work here. I am due to visit the out-patients' dispensary and the gaol at Ibanda. I may see the three accused there, if they have not been moved to Mbarara. At home I shall be able to play golf again with my coaches, Gil and Betty Baird; as I mentioned before he is the executive officer of Mbarara township. One of the greens is adjacent to the Galt Memorial Hall – not that I shall need any reminder of this tour.

[1] Morris *The Uganda Journal* Vol 24 No 1, 4
[2] Lugard *The Rise of our East African Empire* Vol 2, 657
[3] Bell *Glimpses of a Governor's Life* 148

7: IN HIS EXCELLENCY'S CANOE

I am not surprised by your comments in your last letter that Sir Hesketh Bell's collective punishment on the Banyankole was high-handed and arbitrary. The exercise of power in excess of judicial decisions was a feature only of the perceived need to establish law and order in the years up to the 1920s.

It was kind of you to ask after my health. In spite of taking paludrine daily I have had a mild dose of malaria, otherwise I have kept well. We are not greatly troubled by mosquitoes in Mbarara as the township porters keep the grass short and the drains clear. A by-product of this process has been the creation over the years of a nine-hole golf course. This provides the opportunity for some exercise between 4.00pm, when the office closes, and 7.00pm, when it becomes dark. The hours of daylight never vary as we are so close to the equator; I should add that we begin work at 8.00am. We also play tennis on a hard court and the old gaol has been converted to an open-air squash court. I once played David Craxton at midday, of all times; panting with exhaustion I felt that I might share the fate of those early explorers whose untimely deaths were recorded by James Rennell Rodd. More mundanely, mortality can be kept at bay by checking that our cooks are boiling and filtering our water on a regular basis. Soon after I moved into my own bungalow I bought a refrigerator, a significant improvement on storing food in a small 'pantry' clad with fine wire netting and hung in the shade from a tree outside the kitchen. My refrigerator burns paraffin and it can be temperamental. As with paraffin lamps it is essential to trim the wicks regularly, otherwise black pungent smoke curls up to the ceiling. But that slight inconvenience will end when electricity arrives. I had thought that Mbarara would be supplied from Owen Falls, but a small 1,210kw hydro-electric station is being built on the Kagera river at Kikagati. This will also supply the Kyerwa mines, 30 miles to the south in Tanganyika.

Meanwhile I cannot pretend that life is hard in any way, although the dry season in July and August was trying and tempers then tended to fray at the edges. There is a great variety of work. Over the last nine months I have called on Rubambansi the Omugabe, joined in his birthday celebrations, toured in three sazas and visited the Queen Elizabeth National Park with George Sacker, who runs the veterinary department stock farm just outside

Mbarara; he arrived shortly after me. I also lined up the school children in the wrong order for a Commonwealth Day parade and participated in Sir Andrew Cohen's farewell visit.

Before I describe some of these activities, you may like to know that any new ADC is fair game for any new task. Eric Weir called me into his office one morning and said that he wanted me to take charge of the Ankole football team. My protest that I knew nothing of the sport, apart from one or two games when I was a National Service soldier, was of no avail. (Coaching the Ankole VIII – if there had been one – would have been quite a different matter.) The bare-footed Banyankole footballers, he explained, were already proficient. He asked me to organise matches, starting with a team from Masaka. One or two people think that inter-kingdom matches might inhibit rather than promote unity; on the other hand, it must surely be better to promote contact. Eric also asked me to chair a committee to oversee the construction of a grandstand and changing facilities on a new sports ground with money provided by the King George VI Memorial Fund. So there is no end to the variety of work here. One of my tasks in the office is to organise bus services in liaison with the Uganda Transport Company. Another is to hear cases as a third-class magistrate. I now conduct preliminary enquiries into allegations of murder as well as fining people guilty of road traffic offences – hardly comparable activities.

The Omugabe inspects the Ankole football team.

In March the DC sent me one of his hand-written minutes on blue paper. My colleagues and I are likely to receive some of these on Monday mornings as Eric is extremely conscientious, even at weekends. In the week we feel mildly guilty when we are playing off the second tee on the golf course and he is still visibly hard at work by his open windows only a dozen yards away. This particular minute instructed me to make an appointment with the Omugabe's secretary so that I could pay an official call on him. When I duly appeared in his office, the DC's piece of advice for me was "Treat him as a constitutional monarch."

The Omugabe comes to the office occasionally to see the DC and he sits in a finely carved large chair across from the DC's desk. Eric has a very good relationship with him, and also with the Enganzi. They seek his advice and he ensures that all matters are treated consistently and justly. Once, the Omugabe wanted a new car and asked for a large American model similar to one enjoyed by the Omukama of Toro. At least he did not want several Rolls Royces like the Kabaka! Eric persuaded him that the budget would be better served by a cheaper and much more stately Humber limousine.

In due course I drove through a gateway in the elephant-grass stockade around the Mugaba, the name for the palace, which is a tribute to the recent

work of Jack – I described it to you in an earlier letter. I parked to one side of the porte-cochère and the Omugabe's secretary met me at the main door. We turned left towards the Omugabe's study and I found him sitting behind his desk, a large, gentle, benign man, round of face and as tall as any Muhima when he stood to greet me and shake my hand. I had rehearsed the Runyankore greeting. He offered me coffee which was brought in by a servant who kneeled before us. I felt as if I was an interloper, for here was a descendant of the rulers of Ankole who once presided over great herds of long-horned cattle and ordered life according to tradition without the advice or instructions of the white man. We talked through an interpreter and I told the Omugabe about my tours to parts of his kingdom. At the end I informed him that I would do my best to help the Ankole football team and he again shook my hand warmly. As I left I could see our houses in the distance on the next hill. I wondered what he really thinks of us, interlopers with democratic designs, and what an ancestor, Prince Uchunku, thought of his blood brotherhood ceremony with Henry Stanley on 23rd July 1889. "The rite of blood brotherhood began with the laying of a Persian carpet, upon which the Prince and I took our seats cross-legged, with left hands clasped across the knees. The Professors of the Art advanced, and made an incision in each left arm, and then each Professor took a small portion of butter, and two leaflets, which served as platters, mixed it with our blood, and then exchanging the leaves, our foreheads were rubbed with the mixture."[1] I wonder how far my interview with the Omugabe was a modern version of 'blood brotherhood'.

St James' Church at Mbarara.

You asked after our relations with the African and Asian communities. We all work together happily and mix well on special occasions. Recently we celebrated Diwali, the Hindu Festival of Light, when some of the Mbarara shopkeepers entertained us with beer and spicy food in their candlelit shops and houses. The Omugabe's birthday celebrations also brought people together. The first event of the day was a service at St James' Church in the Protestant Mission just outside Mbarara. The DC in his white uniform and helmet waited with the clergy for the Omugabe's arrival in his Humber. He was dressed in his ceremonial robes worn over a suit. These were impressively embroidered and on his head he wore a round hat, more like a top hat without a brim than like a fez, which tapers upwards. His headgear was also decorated; the sacred drums of Ankole, the Bagyendanwa, were carefully embroidered. Then the Omugabe was received at the headquarters of the Ankole Local Government. Accompanied by the DC and the OC Police, he inspected a Guard of Honour of the Uganda Police before receiving a march past by school children outside the palace and attending

a tea party for a cross section of the community; the Catholic White Fathers were among the guests.

Writing of schoolchildren reminds me of an historic task that is always allocated to the junior ADC. Empire Day, 24th May, was chosen by King Edward VII to honour the birthday of his mother, Queen Victoria, and to record the assistance given by the Colonies in the Boer War. This day is still officially Empire Day but is informally referred to as Commonwealth Day. The London Declaration in 1949 confirmed that republics, such an India, could be members of the Commonwealth. In Mbarara the school children parade past the DC who then reads a message from The Queen. So every year the Protestant and Catholic schools produce squads of smartly uniformed children and there is a convention that each denomination leads the parade on alternate years. This means that they have to be lined up beforehand in an appropriate order. I had earlier discussed this with the teachers. It was the Catholics' turn to lead the parade this time. For some reason I then gave the wrong initial instructions and prepared the parade for the Protestants to lead the march past. When I realised what I had done, and remembered the awful years of religious conflicts in the last century, I was in a quandary. Would I, as a Protestant, be accused of favouring my own denomination although, when on safari, my colleagues and I make a point of spending an equal amount of time visiting the different missions? Was there time to reorganise the parade before the DC appeared from his office? In a panic I decided that there might just be time for the children, some hundreds of them, to march into the correct starting positions. They arrived in the right place just one minute before Eric appeared. Afterwards he asked me why they had been late in arriving! I think he must have seen the commands, counter-commands and confusion! Freddie Sheridan asked me in for a drink at lunch time. I think he realised that I needed a stiff gin although I must point out that we do not usually drink at midday in the week. After all it would infringe the bye-law!

I have now completed three tours on my own. My favourite saza so far is Nyabushozi, in the east on the border with Buganda. It stretches from our northern boundary with Toro to well south of the road to Masaka. It is an area of wide open plains and low hills clothed, as far as the eye can see, with long grasses and scrub. It is typically dry acacia savanna with some large expanses of water where the veterinary department have built dams across small river valleys to provide water in the dry season. It is cattle country and the majority of the population are Bahima, mostly tall and bedecked with brightly coloured striped or patterned lengths of cloth which they wind around their waists and throw across their shoulders. The Bahima have a nobility and maintain an aloof ignorance of the reasons for our attempts to restrict their habit of burning the grass, which can lead to soil erosion and loss of fertility. Their womenfolk mainly stay at home where they drink copious amounts of milk and become very fat. The Bahima men seem to fancy very well-rounded women.

A local gombolola chief demonstrates his new motorcycle to some Bahima.

Only the men came to the lukiiko meetings. One evening when walking near the rest camp I met the local gombolola chief demonstrating his brand new motorcycle. Later that evening he persuaded a few Bahima to come and sing around a camp fire at the rest camp, and drink my beer. Their songs, or more correctly recitations, tell of past history, cattle grazing, grass burning, the tsetse fly and their search for better pastures. Their lives are devoted to cattle whose blood and milk are their staple diet.

> The land is beset with flies.
> At Izhumuriro and Nyamiyonga the vultures feast
>   on the slaughtered herds.
> The herds from Obwibura and Nyamiyonga met
>   and died.
> They were skinned by the Muslims and the Bairu.
> Ishingiro and Kyangabukama are infested with flies.
> The Bahima have nowhere to graze their herds.
> Let us leave Magabi and Ntantamuki, they are
>   beset with flies.
> Let us go to other lands.[2]

The tsetse fly is the carrier for sleeping sickness which was a major scourge of the population around the shores of Lake Victoria in the early years of the Protectorate. It also carries trypanosomiasis which kills cattle. The veterinary department is waging a war against the fly; their field officers are in charge of tree clearance because certain types of tree provide a breeding habitat. I met one such officer, Douglas Jones, at his camp out in the bush. Despite his surroundings he was always most elegantly dressed, wearing a cravat and a wide-brimmed hat. He has an aristocratic air and shares a house with Toni Nuti who runs a small hotel on an island in the middle of the Kagera river. Sometimes it is thought necessary also to eliminate game but there is no call for this in Ankole at present. It is a great joy to come across zebra living happily in the bush, miles from a game park; that is until they are shot by a licensed hunter. And there are lion in the south at Sanga – you will recall that I saw one cross the road soon after I arrived. I camped at Sanga during the tour, where there is no rest house, just a flimsy tent shelter for an even more flimsy tent! The gombolola chief arranged for some local people to maintain a camp fire nearby. When I woke in the morning they were still there and the smoke from the embers mingled with the mists of dawn. I thanked them and gave them some beer. I wonder if I would have slept if they had not been there?

The night watchmen and their fire which kept the man-eating lions away, so that I could sleep safely.

Another tour took me to Bunyaruguru saza which I had visited with David Craxton in the early days. Once more the Ruwenzori were hidden in the clouds. However, there was one magical evening in Mbarara when we all rushed round to the north side of our hill – someone had seen the snowy peaks edged against the sky. They crowned the lower dark slopes and although they are some 90 miles away from here, the rare clarity that evening afforded us an amazing and almost eerie experience.

A further and recent excitement was the farewell visit of Sir Andrew Cohen. Last August it was announced that he will become the Permanent UK Representative on the Trusteeship Council at the United Nations when his term of office expires in January next year. This was my first experience of a Governor's visit. Initially the DC, in consultation with the PC, proposed a programme, bearing in mind the content of earlier visits and any specific instructions from HE's Private Secretary. On this occasion the Governor expressed a wish to address the Eishengyero, the council of the Ankole Local Government. He also agreed to visit a fishing village on Lake Mburo in Nyabushozi saza, as well as the stock farm where George Sacker is in charge of improving animal husbandry and research into disease, genetics, and livestock and pasture management. There are some three million head of cattle in Uganda, predominantly zebu, which have humps on their backs, although our Ankole long-horn cattle are a major potential source of income. Presently the Bahima tend to keep their cattle for social and prestige purposes; consequently four scrawny heifers are four times as valuable as a 'pedigree' bull. Last year the value of Uganda's hides and skin exports was about £800,000. The Governor also asked to visit Ntare Secondary School and accepted an invitation to play in a cricket match on the Sunday. The MCC's ground is not quite like that at Lords but the Mbarara Cricket Club carries on the traditions of the game. Once the programme was agreed in principle with the Private Office, the DC made detailed plans and proposed a guest list for a sundowner to be given by the Governor on his last evening. Inevitably the list caused heartache for those who could not be included, emphasis being placed on a fair representation of all the communities. Fortunately, all the administrative officers are invited: but not junior police officers, or the English manager of Barclays Bank!

My involvement centred on the fishing village and I had to go and discuss HE's visit with the saza chief. I am sure that you will be interested to know that one-seventh of the total area of Uganda is water and this provides the potential for the development of a significant fishing industry. This began in 1910 when gill nets were imported for use in catching ngege (a very small fish dried and sold for immediate consumption) in Lake Victoria. In 1935 Lake Nakivali, also in Ankole, was stocked with tilapia; fish ponds as well as dams built for cattle watering are now being stocked. By 1951 the annual value of fish production reached £930,000. At Lake Mburo the game department, which is responsible for fisheries, gives grants for the purchase of outboard motors and these make a substantial difference to productivity. The fishermen construct their own canoes and on these smaller lakes they are only some ten feet long and two feet wide.

The Governor's visit was designed to encourage the fishermen and to celebrate the successful introduction of outboard motors to some of the 'fleet'. The saza chief, aware of the Katunguru regatta which Sir George Duntze had described on my first evening in Mbarara, decided to organise some canoe races. On the day there were plenty of competing two-manned boats lined up near the shore and a large crowd gathered to shout their support. They raced around two stationary boats out in the lake and Freddie Sheridan was chosen to be the judge on the finishing line. Then Lady Cohen presented the prizes and it was a very happy occasion. The saza chief, mindful of the Katunguru tradition of multi-racial competition, challenged the DC and the ADCs to a race. HE immediately insisted on joining in and Eric Weir instructed me to partner Sir Andrew because "you are an oarsman." It was hard to see any connection between a rowing eight, the Cam and these simple boats made of little more than three planks on an African lake. I was initially concerned whether Sir Andrew would actually fit into a canoe. He is large and powerfully built but he just managed to sit behind me and as soon as we began to paddle I realised that his power was greater than mine. So I had to work very hard, taking extra strokes, to keep us on a straight course. Our race was mercifully much shorter than the races which we had witnessed. We did not win. On approaching the shore we were nearly rammed by the saza chief but fortunately for me the Governor was returned to dry land, more or less dry. His participation was rapturously received by the crowd.

At other times on the tour there was a greater formality. With the Omugabe, Sir Andrew inspected a Guard of Honour of the Uganda Police

A collision at the end of the race.
Sir Andrew and I were not the last to finish.

before addressing the Eishengyero. Later that afternoon he received a great welcome at Ntare school. The last of Sir Andrew's engagements was his sundowner for some 70 people representing all aspects of life in Ankole. This was held at the DC's house and the Government House staff were efficient in dispensing drinks and canapés. Towards the end when most people had left, the Governor turned to Freddie Sheridan and me, and Freddie raised the question of the future of the administration in an independent Uganda. Sir Andrew has clearly accelerated the process towards self-government and he sat down with us as soon as he realised our concern. He explained that progress would involve a range of new tasks and possibilities. He admitted that the administration would change but he thought that there would be many tasks for us as advisers and trainers. As our talk went on Eric became somewhat agitated and he must have thought that the Governor might chide him for having such rebellious ADCs! More likely, Ann Weir was concerned that the dinner she was preparing for the Governor might suffer from over-cooking. Sir Andrew was not content to let us go until he felt we were reassured. As at Entebbe, he demonstrated his concern for his staff and maybe he even wished that he had been a district officer himself?

The next day HE left to open the railway extension between Kampala and Kasese. Sixty years ago, when the Protectorate was but two years old, the first rails were laid at Mombasa. Now, at a cost of £5 million, the railway will carry the copper ore that until recently was hidden in the shadowy and mist-laden valleys of the Ruwenzori mountains near Kasese.

I think that I have brought you up to date. I am half way through my first tour and I have enjoyed every minute of it, except for that night at Ibanda. I should add that I have never felt remotely threatened at any other time. The degree of progress we are making was illustrated when I met Grace Ibingira, a Muhima on holiday from university in England. Fluent in English he is clearly one of the future's leaders. I have also met the Omugabe's son, John Barigye, and played tennis with him.

Finally, you will be glad to know that Tosca is behaving very well. She goes everywhere I go, and at home she sits on my veranda with me when I listen to a recording of *Tosca* which my parents sent out for my birthday. If I shut my eyes I can see the castle of St Angelo and, when Tosca has thrown herself over the parapet, there are the hills of southern Ankole in the distance. How fortunate I am to be in Uganda.

[1] Stanley *In Darkest Africa* Vol 2, 349
[2] Ford *The Uganda Journal* Vol 17 No 2, 187

8: A DEMAND FOR SELF-GOVERNMENT – IN 1958!

The second half of my tour seems to have passed very quickly, but as my leave approaches in April I find that I now really do need a holiday. I shall have been in Mbarara for just over two and a half years. My fellow canoe paddler at the Lake Mburo regatta, Sir Andrew Cohen, left Uganda in January 1957 and he was succeeded by Sir Frederick Crawford who arrived a year ago from Kenya, where he had been Deputy Governor. He was previously the Governor of the Seychelles. Unlike Sir Andrew he has served in Africa since being appointed a district officer cadet in Tanganyika in 1929. He was confirmed in his appointment in 1931, the year of my birth! During his service in Tanganyika Sir Frederick was seconded to the East African Governors' Conference which was, I believe, the precursor of the East African High Commission.

You will notice that he began his service as a cadet, as I did. I can now report that I was confirmed in my appointment last September, having passed a further law examination and, presumably, having demonstrated my fitness for permanent employment. How permanent, remains to be seen I celebrated this occasion with my friends in Mbarara and pretentiously sent them all a formal invitation as follows:

The Government of the Protectorate of Uganda

in its most gracious benevolence has deemed it correct and proper to
confirm its servant
Alan James Forward
as a member of its permanent administrative staff.
In celebration of this startling occurrence the presence

of ....
is requested at the official residence of the above
Servant of the said most gracious Government at
8 p.m. on Saturday 21st September, 1957.
Evening Dress and Medals   (R.S.V.P. Your obedient servant.)

The party was not in fact formal and we all enjoyed a supply of red headache-making Belgian Congo wine in demi-johns and a large ham imported from Nairobi.

Perhaps Sir Frederick celebrated his confirmation in a similar way. He arrived in Uganda to the relief of many who hoped that life would be quieter after Sir Andrew's roller-coaster approach to change. There was some initial suspicion in Buganda that Sir Frederick's experience in Kenya and in the Governors' Conference might be an indication that he would be a protagonist for the federation of Kenya, Uganda and Tanganyika. Such fears were quickly dispelled and his initial policy, which reflected views in London, envisaged that a period of stability was required before any further major constitutional changes were made. But the introduction of the ministerial system and the enlargement of the Legislative Council to 60 members in 1955 have produced a momentum which most of us think cannot be slowed. During 1957 there were increasing demands for the direct election of African members of the Legislative Council, or as one poster read in Mbarara, 'We want dilect erections'! I think I told you that 'r's tend to replace 'l's in Runyankore. In April the Council discussed a motion seeking self-government in 1958 – this year! – and independence within the Commonwealth in 1961. Needless to say this motion was defeated, but the Uganda National Congress is becoming more active and more demanding. The Congress makes little impression on the Banyankole who are still more inclined to contemplate their cattle and crops than to pursue politics.

You asked about membership of the Mbarara Club. This is not presently open to Africans or Asians. We have recently debated this issue and the majority take the view that they like to have a place where they can put their feet up and relax amongst their fellows after working all day in the local environment. I would be happy to see a change and it is bound to come as Africanisation proceeds. The first Ugandan district officer, John Kaboha, was appointed in March 1955 and others are being trained at Oxford, Cambridge and London. As Ugandans receive promotion in the departments it will, I think, be inevitable and right that they should be offered membership. It would be highly invidious to exclude Ugandans who become, for example, the district medical officer or a district officer. Whether they will want to take up the offer and share our strange customs is another matter. The Scots, of whom we have a fair number, become quite wild on St Andrew's Night. New Year's Eve is another great celebration and in the Mbarara Sports Club, to give it its full title, the men have to kiss all the ladies at midnight. I have so far avoided Blanche Hall! I cannot over-emphasise the friendliness of all my colleagues; a drink in the club may lead to someone offering eggs and bacon for supper. The bachelors, and there are some six of us, are well entertained, especially at Christmas when no one is left on their own. The curtains in my bungalow were made for me by the wife of one of the teachers at Ntare Secondary School. We help, in return, by running the bar, inviting people to join us on tour at a weekend and, in the case of George Sacker, by providing turkeys for Christmas, on payment of course.

My work continues to be a mixture of touring, court work and a variety of office tasks. When Gil Baird went on home leave I acted as the executive officer of the Mbarara township authority. This brought me into new contacts with more of the Asian shopkeepers, who work extremely hard. Some are clearly quite rich. Amongst my tasks was the supervision of road improvements and the layout of a second roundabout. When Eric Weir returned from local leave I was given 'a rocket' because the new kerbs had not been concreted in the position which he had stipulated.

I do not think that I have explained how the administration co-ordinates the work of all the departmental officers working in the District. The DC chairs meetings of the district team which includes the Enganzi of Ankole and these officers. The task of the team is to co-ordinate Protectorate Government policies and take account of local political circumstances. For example, Ruffi Darlow, our district medical officer, proposed that a new dispensary should be sited according to medical needs, but there were conflicting arguments for building it elsewhere, where the medical case was slightly less strong but where the local people had received less than their fair share of government services.

One day after an unexplained course in Entebbe the DC arranged for steel bars to be fitted to the two filing cabinets in his outer office. At the end of each day these bars have to be lowered through the drawer handles into sockets welded at the base of the cabinets and secured with a large padlock at the top; in the morning they have to be lifted up. Joan Durre, Eric's secretary, found these procedures rather wearing. So I have the task of opening the cabinets in the morning and Eric, usually still the last to leave, secures them in the evening. We later heard that the course he attended had included a

The Ankole football team wearing their new badges.

lecture on protective security by a man from London. One of the wives had worked as a part-time secretary until Joan arrived. Eric gave me the task of ensuring that her bungalow was correctly furnished before her arrival. The public works department normally only provides basic furniture and mattresses. We all have to provide our own curtains, cushions for the cane sofa and chairs and bedding, together with crockery and cooking equipment. However, some of these items are provided for full-time secretaries as an inducement to work up country.

The King George VI Stadium at Kakyeka, near Mbarara – another one of Jack Wyke's buildings.

Sir Frederick Crawford made his first official visit to Ankole at the end of last year. An important function, especially for me, was the opening by the Governor of the new sports ground and grandstand. The Ankole Sports and Welfare Association, of which I am the chairman, planned the opening and I had quite an argument with Basil Bataringaya, a teacher and an up-and-coming leader. He was reluctant to agree to name the stadium after King George VI. I firmly explained that the funds had been subscribed by many people throughout the world to commemorate the late King and that it would be wrong not to use his name. He agreed without any rancour. A football match was arranged with some timed cycle races at half-time. The Ankole football team had earlier had some success in matches with teams from Buganda and Kigezi and we designed a badge for the team, featuring the sacred drums of Ankole, the Bagyendanwa, crossed spears and a lion. We ordered a supply through the Crown Agents and the parcel arrived at the post office about half an hour before the opening ceremony. Fortunately our team included two tailors who somehow swiftly stitched the badges to the team's shirts. We had arranged for a detachment of The King's African Rifles to be present with their band and both teams were lined up for inspection by the

Governor and the Omugabe before the kick-off. Quite like Wembley! On an earlier occasion we arranged a game between the Banyankole and the British. Sportingly, the Omugabe, who is not a natural athlete, played in goal. His skills were not greatly stretched because our barefooted opponents ran rings around us for most of the time. They won easily and the afternoon was a very pleasant, friendly and successful occasion.

Life is not all fun and games but you may think it is when I tell you that on my local leave I visited the Murchison Falls National Park where I met up with some of my 1955 colleagues at Paraa Lodge on the Nile. I drove to Fort Portal and stayed a night with David Pasteur. He could not come to the Park so I drove on alone to Hoima, the headquarters of the third Western Province kingdom, Bunyoro Kitara, to give it its full name. In the days of Kabalega, the uncle of the present Omukama, Tito Gafabusa Winyi IV, the kingdom is said to have extended from Tanganyika to Lake Rudolf in the north of Kenya and from Lake Naivasha in the Rift Valley to the Ituri forest in the Congo. As I think I told you, the Banyoro and Baganda were in conflict when the British arrived. The Banyoro came off worst and they have ever since had a grievance because certain of their sazas, or counties, were given to Buganda. They are now known as the 'Lost Counties'.

The Murchison Falls Park lies partly in Bunyoro and partly in Acholi in the Northern Province. Altogether it covers 12,000 square miles and bestrides the Nile, which I had to cross by means of a small ferry to reach Paraa Lodge on the northern bank in Acholi. There I met Hubert Allen from Gulu and

The Nile plunging through a gorge, only 19 feet wide, at the Murchison Falls.

John Cleave from Karamoja; Robin Palmer came from Jinja and Edward Cunningham from Soroti. There are splendid views of the vast river winding its way towards Lake Albert with the mountains in the Belgian Congo making a low and distant backcloth. Elephant graze around the lodge; crocodile and hippopotamus infest the river. A highlight of our visit was a trip by launch to the Murchison Falls. These were discovered in 1864 by Samuel Baker and his wife who arrived in Uganda from the north. He named the falls after the President of the Royal Geographical Society at the time. Two park rangers were in charge of quite a flimsy craft and we passed close to large numbers of hippo and hove to within a few feet of an enormous crocodile which was basking on a sand bank with its viciously toothed jaws wide open. Herds of buffalo and elephant grazed near the water. Later we could see clouds of spray rising into the air above the falls, a mile or two away. Along the banks the rangers pointed out goliath heron, fish eagles, Egyptian geese, tree-duck, darters, kingfishers and weaver birds. We had assumed that we would view the falls from the river but after a while, with the waters becoming increasingly choppy, we moored at a very small jetty on the southern bank. It soon became clear that we were going to walk along and up the rock face to the top. We were greatly relieved when one of the rangers produced a rifle from the launch and he led the way. Thus, after all those years in which the exploring white men led columns of porters through the unknown, here were we following the lead of our Acholi ranger. It was the middle of the day, the heat was intense and the rocky path a test of balance.

Once again we were following in the footsteps of Winston Churchill. "At length we turned a corner and came face to face with the Falls. They are wonderful to behold, not so much because of their height – though that is impressive – but because of the immense volume of water which is precipitated through such a narrow outlet. Indeed, seeing the great size of the river below the Falls, it seemed impossible to believe that it was wholly supplied from this single spout. In clouds of rainbow spray and amid thunderous concussions of sound we set to work to climb the southern side of the rock wall, and after an hour achieved the summit. It was possible to walk to within an inch of the edge and, lying on one's face with a cautious head craned over, to look actually down upon the foaming hell beneath. The narrowness of the gorge at the top had not been overstated. I doubt whether it is fifteen feet across from sheer rock to sheer rock. Ten pounds, in fact, would throw an iron bridge across the Nile at this point. But it is evident that the falling waters must have arched and caved away the rock below their surface in an extraordinary degree, for otherwise there could not possibly be room for the whole river to descend."[1]

An iron footbridge now spans the gorge and the view from its centre straight down into the boiling cauldron of water was quite unnerving. I did not linger long upon this lightweight structure. I am not sure how far a skilled long jumper jumps, but the chasm at its narrowest is in fact about 19 feet wide. Acholi warriors used to jump it, from the slightly higher northern side. At least if one failed one would be pulped before the jaws of the crocodiles waiting below closed around whatever was left. You will know from this letter that I did not try!

So Uganda has two of the finest tourist attractions in the world, the Mountains of the Moon and the Murchison Falls, but there are others, albeit smaller. South of Mbarara on the Kagera River lives Toni Nuti, whom I mentioned in an earlier letter, and I recently had the chance to stay a night at her home which is also a small hotel. When I arrived I found this petite woman supervising workers who were laying the concrete foundations for some new bedrooms; and knitting! As she walked amongst them she was busy on a new pullover or something. Her home is not on the river bank; it is on an island in the river reached by little more than a fallen tree trunk. Everything, including the cement and building blocks, has to be carried over. Her home is a replica of an English cottage; oak furniture and chintz curtains and cushions abound. All of this contrasts with the wild animals which are mainly kept in her zoo outside. Some come in. She has rescued many injured animals and occasionally a passing hippo tours the island. Toni came to East Africa from Italy at the age of 17 and married a miner in Tanganyika. She was one of the very few women who was a white hunter. Once she had a burst appendix in West Nile district and had to be carried in a litter for 30 miles to the nearest village. Her companion then had to walk the same distance to a telephone. Eventually she was rescued by car and boat and made a total recovery! Later she managed a tea plantation at Masaka and helped in the opening of Paraa Lodge. It is no wonder that her African helpers and her many visitors reflect the affection she has for life.

I think that you may well conclude that I shall be very sad when the time comes to leave Ankole and all its cheerful peoples. I have been very lucky to begin my career here and work for Eric Weir who sets such a good example, and who is so well regarded by the Omugabe and by the leaders of the local government. He is for them, as for us, a hard task-master but they and we respect him for his just advice and high standards of administration. I have also had excellent colleagues in Russel Barty and Freddie Sheridan. We have recently been joined by Beadon Dening who was formerly in the Sudan Civil Service and whom I had the pleasure of conducting around the resettlement areas in Mitoma. He came out to join me when I was already some days into

The iron bridge built since Winston Churchill's visit.

The Nile becomes a foaming torrent below the bridge.

a tour and I came back one evening, hot and dusty, to find him at the rest camp, immaculately turned out. Prior to the Sudan he had served in the Royal Navy during the war, I think on midget submarines, but he never speaks of those experiences.

One thing I shall never forget; the schoolchildren. Their keenness to learn in their bare-walled classrooms and their exuberance as they play make-shift games of football are amazing. Their teachers are devoted to their task and Uganda owes much to the missionaries, the first of whom arrived in the late 1870s, since they and not the Government introduced education. Some came in response to Henry Stanley's letter to *The Daily Telegraph* in 1875. "But, oh that some pious, practical missionary would come here! What a field and a harvest ripe for the sickle of Civilisation! . . . It is the practical Christian tutor, who can teach people how to become Christians, cure their diseases, construct dwellings, understand and exemplify agriculture, and turn his hand to anything, like a sailor – this is the man who is wanted. Such an one if he can be found would become the saviour of Africa."[2] I shall also not forget one of them, Dr Archie Stanley-Smith, who lives with his wife in a very simple home close to St James' Church. They have occasionally invited me to supper.

I shall be flying home from Entebbe in April and the BOAC Argonaut aircraft will stop at Khartoum and Rome. I gather that I shall have good views of the Alps, only 3,000 feet below, if the weather is clear. I have received permission to sell my Vanguard pick-up to an African trader and once home I am taking delivery of Eric Weir's 1947 two-and-a-half litre Jaguar for £120. I shall be due about five months' leave and I will be given my next posting whilst I am at home in New Malden. But Africa will not be forgotten for I have agreed to escort some Uganda chiefs during part of their visit to Nottingham where they will see how the Raleigh bicycles, which are so common here, are made. I expect the designers would be amazed if they could see the uses to which their bicycles are put here, carrying many large bunches of bananas or bedsteads or bundles of firewood; or all of these together. I never saw anything quite like this when cycling past the Odeon cinema to school along the A3. It will be so strange to see the normal sights of English daily life again.

[1] Churchill *My African Journey* 165
[2] Stanley *The Daily Telegraph* 15 November 1875, 5

9: THE ACHOLI DANCE FOR THE QUEEN MOTHER

I had an excellent leave and I was glad to hear later that you had enjoyed our visit to the rowing regatta on Lake Llanberis. I shall have to tell Eric that the only thing which went wrong with the Jaguar was the failure of the condenser on our way to Wales. In August I drove my parents, Ronald and Ann around the western highlands of Scotland in perfect weather. Very sadly, I had to sell the Jaguar as it was too long for our garage at home.

Eric Weir's Jaguar, my parents, Ronald and Ann in north-west Scotland.

I am now living in Kampala and working as an assistant resident in Buganda. You were right; it was quite likely that I would be moved from one kingdom to another. The Kabaka's kingdom is divided into four parts: Mubende, where there is the territorial dispute with Bunyoro over the 'Lost Counties', Masaka and East and West Mengo. Each is staffed by a senior assistant resident and one, or at the most two, assistant residents. I work in West Mengo and John Gotch is in charge. On my arrival in Kampala I was invited to stay with the Resident, Tony Richards, who is the equivalent of a provincial commissioner. The title resident was introduced to replace the title provincial commissioner in Buganda in 1944 by Sir Charles Dundas, the Governor at that time, who thereby reduced the Protectorate Government's influence in Buganda. In doing so he maintained the earlier policy of indirect rule under Lugard instead of working towards the creation of a unitary state. On my first evening before dinner, my host walked me to and fro across the spacious lawns surrounding his large house in a very pleasant leafy part of Kampala. He explained that my role would be much more that of an adviser than an administrator. He told me that I must not expect to oversee the work of the Buganda Government chiefs, as I had done in Ankole. My task would be more akin to that of a representative, even a diplomat. He expects his staff to help him convey the Protectorate Government's policies to the people of Buganda. He confessed that the deportation and return of the Kabaka had not made this any easier, particularly for some of his staff who, in accordance with the policy of the time, had been unequivocal in explaining that the Kabaka would never return. When he did return his popularity was increased, whereas it had begun to wane before the deportation.

I was generally aware of these circumstances and quickly found out that the Kabaka and his retinue are in many ways most impressive. It so happened that while I was staying in the Residency, Tony Richards and his wife Babs held a sundowner for the Kabaka, some of his staff and some of the Asian residents of Kampala. His Highness arrived late and I was briefly introduced to him by the Resident. As I noted at the GH garden party in 1955, he has all the poise and confidence of a Cambridge graduate, Guards officer and a king. Somehow one is aware that here is a man whose ancestors had long ruled with authority. Stanley suggested that Buganda "was first peopled by immigrants from the north, about the thirteenth or fourteenth century."[1] He recorded the names of all the 35 kabakas, beginning with Kintu, "a very respectable list of kings for a country in Central Africa, and proves Uganda to be a monarchy of no mean antiquity."[2] I had quite a long talk with Edward Ndaula, the Buganda Government's information officer. Also a Cambridge graduate, he was both friendly and assertive of Buganda's place in Uganda, even in the world! He has a remarkably well-polished English accent. The Resident introduced the Kabaka to as many people as possible, but afterwards Babs made the point that King Freddie, as he is less formally known, is surrounded almost exclusively by aged acolytes who seek to preserve his kingdom and their own positions. She wished that he could spend more time with younger people outside his immediate circle.

I moved into a modern flat opposite the Speke Hotel in the middle of Kampala, which means 'the place of the Uganda Kob antelope'. Rome has only seven hills, Kampala has some 20. Of these Mengo hill is the most important in the eyes of the Baganda as it is crowned by the Lubiri, a large enclosed area which includes the Twekobe, the Kabaka's palace, an older palace, schools and offices.

I soon found out that the Baganda are daily becoming more sensitive about the position of the Kabaka in an independent Uganda. They declined to participate at the end of last year in the direct elections to the Legislative Council. Elsewhere the secret ballot was achieved by each voter putting a slip of paper in one of the separate boxes for each candidate, bearing his name and his symbol, for example an elephant or a banana. At their meetings candidates explained their symbols to the electorate. This procedure successfully helped those who cannot read or write to cast their votes. The Governor made an important statement at the opening of the new Legislative Council last November. As well as reassuring the traditional leaders he announced the terms of reference of a Constitutional Committee. These include the necessity to provide adequate and effective representation of the non-African communities. Then in February this year the Governor appointed the 15 members of the Committee. The Chairman is the Hon JV Wild, the Administrative Secretary. Most of the members are politicians drawn from all parts of the country, including Milton Obote who is forming a new party, the Uganda People's Congress. The membership also includes two Asians, CK Patel and HK Jaffa, together with the historian, Kenneth Ingham of Makerere University. They are currently touring the country but the Buganda Government, having refused to propose any members for service on the Committee, has boycotted it. Nevertheless the Committee is taking oral and written submissions from individual Baganda. The five Buganda seats in the Legislative Council remain empty.

As an assistant resident I have a limited role. We have to obtain the agreement of a saza chief before we can go on tour in a saza. This is not usually refused, rather letters proposing a visit are just never answered. On one occasion when I did address a meeting in a gombolola hall, I noticed that the tables and chairs for the chief and me were placed, unusually, at floor level rather than on a dais at the end of the hall above which hung a large photograph of the Kabaka. I had taken Tosca with me; she loathes staying in Kampala as much as I do. Noting my demotion she moved to the centre of the dais and sat immediately below the photograph! No one seemed to mind, not even the Muslims!

My days in the office are rather dull but the weekends provide opportunities. I am occasionally invited to lunch by Hubert Allen's parents, John and Wink, at Makerere College. He was a provincial commissioner in Tanganyika and is now, in his retirement, the Warden of University Hall and the Director of the Institute of Swahili Research. Such occasions are stimulating for they always invite a good mixture of students and people from various walks of life. Conversation flows fast – woe betide anyone who does not utter! The College began its life in 1922 as a technical college and became a medical school two years later. In 1937 it became a centre for higher education in East Africa and achieved its present status as a university college of London University in 1949. It is situated on yet another of Kampala's hills and its modern buildings, which cost £1 million, are as good as their equivalent in England. There is a splendidly optimistic atmosphere at the College; students come to study from all parts of East Africa. Their number include Asians and a few Europeans. It is an institution which seeks to break down tribalism. Students live in six 'halls' which are organised along Oxbridge college lines, each has a 'High Table' and all compete in sports.

Sometimes I escape up country at weekends, returning through the dawn on a Monday morning, my headlights searching for the best part, or on occasions any part, of the murram road until the first shafts of light come from the east. Then the smoke from the roofs of homesteads rises through the mists in the valleys. On a visit to Mbarara I found that Eric Weir had gone on leave and that he will have a new posting on his return. On hearing of his departure the Enganzi wept, such was his respect for Eric. I also met one of the new Ugandan ADCs, Frank Kalimuzo, and had an enjoyable evening with him and his colleagues. He is now the Secretary of the Constitutional Committee. Clearly he is on the fast track and rightly so. Yet you may be surprised to know that as recently as last August another group of new British district officers arrived after a three-week voyage on the *Kenya Castle*. In the course of lunch with Charles Hartwell, the Chief Secretary and the Governor's deputy, one of them, Garth ap Rees, remarked that his future would be rather limited. "What do you mean?" bellowed Hartwell, a man known for his temper and tendency to throw his telephone out of the window when annoyed. Humbly, Garth said that he thought that independence must come within six years. "I've been in East Africa for 15 years and I intend to remain here for the next 15 years," replied Kali Charlie who thumped the table and spilt his pink gin. (Kali is the Swahili word for angry.) The Minister for Local Government, Lachlan Boyd, took Garth to one side and said, "What on earth did you say to him?" Garth told him and Lachlan replied, "Young man, there is a faint possibility that you are perspicacious but, my God, you're a tactless young bugger." Nobody believes that the Chief Secretary will be here in fifteen years time and I decided to send a minute to him.

In my minute I suggested that Uganda's future as a unitary state was under threat from the growth of tribalism, particularly from Buganda's feudalism and tendency towards separatism. I argued that the development of political parties must be encouraged and that this could be achieved by the government announcing a realistic timetable for independence. I proposed that we should set a target for self-government in 1963 and independence in 1966. It is the convention here when submitting files or papers to higher authority to send them via one's immediate superiors. I addressed the Chief Secretary 'ufs the Resident', 'ufs the Senior Assistant Resident West Mengo'. There are two interpretations of 'ufs'. One is 'under flying seal', the other 'under forward seal'. The Resident read my paper and called me to his office. He said that he understood my argument that it is necessary to encourage latent politicians and assure them of our intention to turn Uganda into a unitary and democratic state, rather than to leave them floundering in feudal societies. I had also argued that setting a target would concentrate the minds of all the people on the prospect of our departure. However, he thought that my arguments would be swept aside were he to send my paper to the Chief Secretary. Rather reluctantly I acquiesced out of respect for the Resident, who is in an unenviable position; caught between the Baganda and the Governor.

There are some compensations in Kampala. Soon after I arrived I was asked if I would like to read the English news on Radio Uganda. Fred Hills, who is on secondment from the BBC to the Information Department, gave me a test and some advice. The essential requirement is to be very emphatic when necessary, otherwise the radio waves tend to dull one's delivery. I go down to the studios once or twice a week in the early evening and I am then given the news and a limited time in which to check the pronunciation of local names. I enjoy this as I know that I will actually be speaking to some of my up-country friends. So you see, one may be a football club manager in one place and a news reader in another!

Much more excitingly, Her Majesty The Queen Mother visited Uganda in February this year and I was given two tasks. One was to assist the Information Department to look after visiting journalists and photographers from many countries. In spite of very careful briefings and assurances that they would comply with instructions to remain in specific positions at a whole range of functions, they broke ranks as soon as the action began. As individuals they were delightful, especially Audrey Russell of the BBC; but in a bunch they were uncontrollable. The second task was to help stage a tattoo in honour of Her Majesty at Nakivubo Stadium in Kampala. I had been appointed secretary to the stadium management committee on my arrival, another one of those jobs for a junior administrative officer. Her Majesty had previously visited Uganda with The Duke of York in 1925. The Duke and Duchess embarked in *SS Samuel Baker* at a tiny quay on Lake Albert and sailed down the White Nile to Nimule. My responsibility, 34 years later, was to liaise with the Kampala Acholi Association and arrange for their Larakaraka dancers to perform to an exciting rhythm played on drums and calabashes. My major concern was they would all be ready for collection by the transport which I organised and that they would conclude their performance in the allotted ten minutes. Normally they dance for hours! I am sure that I could not have stopped them if they had wanted to continue. Fortunately their leader, an inspector in the Uganda Police, was firmly in control of them. The Acholi have a reputation as hunters and soldiers and have given outstanding service in the Uganda battalion of The King's African Rifles in war and peace. Later there was one exceptionally poignant moment when the lights in the stadium were dimmed and the battalion marched past the royal box where the remaining lights glistened upon Her Majesty's tiara. From across the stadium I could see Her Majesty and she must have been greatly touched listening to the soldiers singing 'Kingi Georgi Tumpe Salama KAR' to the tune of *Clementine*:

> The KAR salutes Kingi Georgi
> Hulai! Hulai! Hulai!
> The KAR salutes Kingi Georgi
> Hulai! Hulai! Hulai!
> We fought until the war was over
> From Europe to Africa.
> The KAR salutes Kingi Georgi
> Hulai! Hulai! Hulai!

These strong and well-drilled men sang the words 'Kingi Georgi' quietly and affectionately as they marched below her and I, among many I suspect, had to wipe away my tears. Later Her Majesty visited all the provinces of Uganda. In the course of this tour Her Majesty flew over Lake Albert and the Nile, the scene of her journey on the *Samuel Baker* all those years ago. She referred to this in a speech at Paraa Lodge and mentioned that she had been able to see the beautiful country of northern Uganda, stretching away from the mountains of the West Nile district eastwards towards the heights of Karamoja. At Gulu she saw the Acholi dancers perform the famous Bwola dance. She was photographed, a small figure in an elegant jewelled gown amongst these massive men in their animal skin costumes and feathered head-dresses.

Her Majesty's visit was an outstanding success. After it was all over I concluded that I preferred working with the Acholi than with the pack of journalists. When I drove Audrey Russell to the airport she was amused to hear that I am a news reader, and that I was trained by the BBC. Apart from these excitements I have found life in Kampala rather dull. My golf is not up to a standard for the Kampala golf club and I have not joined the Kampala Club, as I am often away at weekends. One compensation is the Chez Josef restaurant where I and some colleagues have enjoyed one or two excellent Tournedos Rossini.

I have recently paid another visit to Kigezi down in the south-west. This time I drove beyond the district headquarters of Kabale over some amazing mountain roads and down to Kisoro, very near the border with Ruanda. My aim was to climb up the slopes of an extinct volcano to see the gorillas. Muhavura, 13,540 feet, means 'he who shows the way'. It is certainly visible from afar, like a giant signpost. I stayed at the Travellers' Rest, a small hotel run by Walter Baumgartel who arranges trackers and guides. Robin Tamplin, another district officer who had arrived in late 1955 without attending a 'Devonshire' course, had planned to join me, but could not take leave at the time. So after a night of rest I left early in the morning with a local guide, Walter's advice ringing in my ears: "When you meet a gorilla, you crouch, bow your head and on no account move or make a noise." He advised me that the most likely place to find the gorillas at that time was in the col between Muhavura and Mgahinga, the next in the line of five volcanoes. The latter is "the 'Hill of Cultivation' for peasants used to cross its lower slopes on their way to the blacksmiths of the impenetrable forest from whom alone they could obtain hoes with which to cultivate the ground."[3] To the west of Mgahinga there is a third extinct volcano, Sabinio. These three peaks lie east–west along our border with Ruanda; Sabinio also marks the meeting point of the Ruanda, Uganda and Congo boundaries. There are more volcanoes in the Congo; collectively they are all called the Virunga mountains. Two in the Congo smoke and smoulder continually and one, Nyamulagira, erupted in 1938.

We had a very steep and straight ascent up to the col and there my guide suggested that we might find these mighty animals on the slopes of Mgahinga. He found some evidence of their recent presence and tracked them for a while. The trail then went cold; it was perhaps too much to hope for success in only one day. Struggling through the dense vegetation we climbed up to the rim of Mgahinga, 11,400 feet, and arrived as the mists spread up from below. We could just see the bottom of the crater which was green and yellow, a bog rather than the lake which I expected to find. The mosses no doubt concealed a pit of unknown depth. We remained on the rim, as it would have been foolhardy to try and descend the very steep sides of the crater. It was an eerie experience sitting where once, 100,000 years ago, molten lava had first erupted. Who knows when such a volcano might become active once again? Nevertheless, it was with great regret that I realised that we had to make a start down to the col. As we looked south-east from the col the land falls away towards Lake Ruhondo which drains to the Kagera river and then through Lake Victoria to the Nile. As the Kagera is the largest river to flow into Lake Victoria, you may agree that the source of the Nile lies in the country we saw below us rather than at Jinja. I could have stayed in the col for hours contemplating the landscape but we had to continue down to the Travellers' Rest. My guide, who spoke some English, was a considerate companion throughout. On the way up he seemed to know when I was about to run out of breath, and we had amazing views over Kigezi and the 'impenetrable forest' lying between us and Lake Edward. We had a beer in the hotel and he left to return to his nearby home to await the next visitor seeking an audience with the gorillas. Their numbers can only be estimated owing to the dense vegetation throughout their environment. My failure to find them was balanced by the fear of finding them, not that they are a threat if properly approached.

On my return to Kampala I began a new task; numbering the population. The Central Government conducts a census every ten years and I was given the responsibility for organising the census in West Mengo, excluding Kampala, but including the shanty town area around it known as the Kibuga. In 1948 the total population of Uganda was just under 5 million. The organisation of a census requires much detailed planning and the training of enumerators who each have to be given clearly designated areas. Additionally, there is a need to explain the reasons for a census to the people and this has given me the chance to go on tour. Some Ugandans suspect that a census is a means of increasing taxation, others are just more generally fearful and unable to understand that population studies are a necessary part of government planning. In Buganda there is growing hostility to the Central Government as the people await the report of the Constitutional Committee. They held their first meeting two days ago and they are planning to visit every district. It is unlikely that their report will be published much before the end of the year.

10: IN THE DISTRICT COURT OF MASAKA
AT BUTENGA

BUTENGA
7th August 1959

You will know from my last letter that I was not entirely content in Kampala, with its urban way of life and the difficulties of dealing with some of the Baganda chiefs, who effectively prevented me from touring their counties. Here, in the Masaka District of Buganda, there has been an outbreak of intimidation and arson. I am now camping at a gombolola chief's headquarters and, in the circumstances, I did not wait to secure his agreement to set up my tent and fly the Union Jack in his compound!

I did not have time to write to you two months ago after Tony Richards called me into his office. He told me that I must move the next day to Masaka to work with Michael Wright, who is acting as the Senior Assistant Resident while Graham Moss is on leave for four months. The Resident explained that he needed to maintain two officers at Masaka because of the worsening relations between the Central Government and the Kabaka's Government, and the likelihood of a breakdown in law and order. This sounded rather grim, more so than the one occasion when I had to go with a police detachment to the down-town market area of Kampala when there was a threat of politically inspired disturbances. On that occasion I was acting on the orders of John Gotch and I was instructed to be ready to read the riot act, literally, prior to any use of firearms by the police to disperse a mob. Fortunately on that Saturday afternoon the ardour of the protesters was cooled by a typically sudden rainstorm! So it was with some foreboding, and maybe hope for continuous rain, that I packed up my belongings in my flat in Kampala. Once clear of the capital and its shanty towns, I was soon driving across the equator into the lush Masaka countryside. Masaka is some 90 miles to the south-west of Kampala and close to the shores of Lake Victoria. I often used to drive through the town when I was living at Mbarara, but I rarely stopped for more than a meal or petrol. Once I stayed at an old, untidily thatched hotel outside Masaka where, unusually, there were horses available for riding. (The tsetse fly usually inhibits such activity in Uganda.) The undulating Buganda countryside here is less dramatic than the hills and plains of Ankole, but there are views from the flat-topped hills of Lake Victoria which covers 26,000 square miles; the world's second biggest lake. There are also many more people and much more evidence of material progress.

Speke had travelled through this area. "There was no want of food here, for I never saw such a profusion of plantains [green bananas] anywhere. They were literally lying in heaps on the ground, though the people were brewing pombe [beer] all day and cooking them for dinner every evening."[1] Now the farmers' large houses with corrugated-iron roofs are signs of prosperity. There are coffee-processing factories in or near a few of the trading centres along this road. Some are owned by the Asians whose forefathers enterprisingly initiated the development of Uganda's economy in the early years of this century. In 1957 new legislation enabled the local farmers to form co-operatives and build their own factories. The Asians continue to own most of the shops in Masaka and many in the villages in the surrounding countryside. The Resident warned me before I left Kampala that the Uganda National Movement and the Uganda National Congress were planning to organise a boycott of all non-African traders and transport operators.

I reported to Michael Wright on my arrival and he showed me to my rather dreary modern house. He is fluent in Luganda and often spends his weekends recording the early history of Buganda by talking with some of the oldest people in the district. Neither he nor I was too surprised when the boycott started, shortly after my arrival. Almost immediately there were reports of arson as the leaders of the boycott wreaked their vengeance on people who continued to buy their provisions from the Asians. Most who did so were immigrants from Ruanda who came to Buganda to find menial work. Their thatched huts are highly vulnerable to stealthy fire-raisers in the middle of the night. The situation deteriorated quite quickly and extra police were posted into the district, which was declared a 'disturbed area' under the police ordinance. Public meetings are now restricted to 25 persons, a curfew has been imposed at night and I am gazetted as a second-class magistrate. Michael Wright sent me here to Butenga, about 12 miles north-west of Masaka; it is one of the worst trouble spots.

I had very little notice but there was time to buy a hammer, a few nails, a pulley and some rope. I packed my law books, a Union Jack and all the usual touring kit, and on my arrival here I set up my tent in the shade of the trees in the chief's compound. After telling the chief, who has a haughty indifference, that my purpose is to assist in the restoration of law and order, I went to a local mission school to buy a slim 25-foot eucalyptus pole from one of the teachers, who has a small plantation of these trees at his house. The chief was not particularly happy when he saw me hoisting the Union Jack aloft in his compound; even when I told him that it was there on the instructions of the Resident.

While the Kabaka and his ministers have condemned the use of violence, they have not opposed the boycott. The chief is therefore not particularly helpful though most Baganda do not like violence. His co-operation certainly does not extend to arranging supplies of food for my camp as was the custom in Ankole. Things have changed since Speke's day. When news of his arrival in Buganda reached the Kabaka, Speke was told, "for the future you must buy no more food. At every place that you stop for the day the officer in charge will bring you plantains, for such are the laws of the land when a king's guest travels in it."[2] I am certainly not a guest.

Given these circumstances, you will be glad to know that I am not alone. As I sit writing this letter beside my tent, I can see a 37-strong platoon of the police special force. They are under the command of Assistant Superintendent Len Taylor, formerly of the Palestine and Metropolitan Police. They have radio operators who, using the call-sign 'Eagle One', maintain contact with their headquarters in Kampala, and they are equipped with three rifles, four greener (shot) guns and two gas guns. None has been used so far. The police were immediately effective in imposing the curfew by maintaining irregular nightly patrols. Although Len and I are camped within shouting distance of each other and need to exchange information, we nevertheless maintain a certain 'distance' – being prosecutor and magistrate respectively. A company of the 4th Battalion, The King's African Rifles, is stationed at Masaka and patrols the district, literally showing the flag as the Union Jack is carried at the head of swiftly marching patrols both by day and by night. Michael Wright visits me occasionally to tell me of the latest arrangements for co-ordinating police and army efforts to apprehend the arsonists. He also told me that the Kabaka has complained to the Resident about my Union Jack. Normally it is only flown at our offices at Kampala, Masaka and Mubende. The Resident also flies the Union Jack on his car when travelling in Buganda, except when he is at Entebbe where he orders his driver to remove the flag, in deference to the Governor. You may think that flying the flag above my tent in the depths of the Kabaka's kingdom is an unnecessary gesture. Certainly, when Lugard arrived in Kampala in December 1880, he made no mention of a flag, "understanding that it means that they give away their country."[3] We are in a somewhat stronger position than Lugard, who chose "a pair of comparatively sound melton cords, which for ten years had accompanied my travels; and a jacket of a sleeping suit, fitted with brass buttons"[4] in order to impress the Kabaka. Now we are deliberately emphasising the Central Government's duty to maintain law and order, a fragile but vital condition, as we prepare Uganda for independence. It is clearly going to be difficult to persuade the

Baganda to co-operate with the rest of the country.

I have spent most of today walking in the villages, where I have seen more evidence of the arsonists' cowardly work. Arson has in the past usually been the outcome of drunken disputes, but this campaign has a much more sinister purpose. I shall not easily forget the fear in the eyes of one poor man whose thatched roof had been ignited in a flash during the night. He and his family had escaped but their few belongings lay charred within the blackened walls, now open to the ever-blue sky; dreadful jagged emblems of insecurity amidst the homely clearing in the green banana trees. It is no wonder that most people in Uganda try to provide themselves with the security of a corrugated-iron roof as soon as they can raise the money.

The police have been very active, and a number of people have already been charged. I have heard a succession of cases, sitting in the chief's lukiiko hall, but taking care not to presume to use the dais. This time Tosca is more discreet and stays in the tent. Being gazetted as a second-class magistrate, I have additional powers, including the authority to send offenders to prison for up to seven years. Some of the cases have been relatively minor, such as being an idle and disorderly person, contrary to Section 162 of the penal code. Others have concerned the possession of articles used in witchcraft, threatening violence, obstructing a police officer, corruption of a public officer and, worst of all, arson. Last week I sentenced Stephen Kalanzi to seven years' imprisonment. Tall, thin and with somewhat threatening eyes, he had been clearly identified by three witnesses who had seen him in the light of a blazing house. There had been a history of trouble between Kalanzi and the complainant; Kalanzi had threatened the latter after he chose not to support the boycott. The seriousness of depriving a man of his freedom for such a large part of his life weighed on me. On the other hand, the collapse of law and order through intimidation is too frightful to contemplate in a country where the people are mainly content and usually respect their chiefs, the law and us. Some people at home may question why a young officer should have the responsibility of passing such a sentence, but a large part of our year's training in Oxford was devoted to law. We were fortunate that our tutor, Rupert Cross, though blind, had a vivid perception of the essential knowledge for our work out here and a talent for presenting it with clarity and occasionally a touch of broad humour. Then of course people at home also need to realise that there are very few of us out here: Michael and I are trying to maintain law and order in a district of some 400,000 people spread over nearly 4,000 square miles! There is no doubt that the security of people's daily lives is in a fragile condition. The rule of law and order, once lost, is not easily regained.

The Governor, under the powers vested in him by the deportation ordinance, has just ordered the removal of some of the instigators of the boycott to remote parts of the country, and we now expect that there will be a reduction in acts of violence. One part of the district, the Sese Islands out in Lake Victoria, remains unstained by all this uncharacteristic spoiling of Uganda's reputation as a land of co-operation, colour and cheerfulness. I was visiting Bukakata, a small village on the lake shore, recently and I noticed a crowd around one of the buildings by a small jetty, where a motor launch was moored. I approached the building and found that His Highness the Kabaka was present and I was told that he was staying in the area for a few days. I think he has a palace or hunting lodge in the north-east part of the district. He must have been as surprised to see me as I was to see him. We had a short conversation. Perhaps in the tradition of his warrior ancestors he asked me, "What is your strength here?" I replied, "Two", meaning Michael and myself. If I had added the numbers of police and army I could have replied 100 or so. You might think this a small number compared to the Kabaka's 400,000 subjects in the district. Perhaps mindful of Babs Richards' suggestion that the Kabaka should meet more people and, in the Ankole tradition of informality, I asked the Kabaka if he would like to come to drinks at my Masaka house the next day in the evening. He graciously accepted and my immediate problem was to gauge the numbers of his retinue who might also come. I told Michael Wright about my invitation. I think that he was a bit surprised because assistant residents in Buganda do not normally ask 'the King' in for a drink! I asked the heads of departments in Masaka to attend and on the night we duly awaited his arrival. Needless to say he was late but it was a pleasant evening and the Kabaka spoke to most people. He did not complain of my flying the flag out at Butenga – but it was just as well that I did not invite him to my tent!

Subsequently Michael received a request from the Resident for one of us to conduct Martin Flegg, the Kabaka's British solicitor, around the disturbed areas. As Michael was due to be elsewhere I waited for the solicitor to arrive at our office in Masaka and was rather surprised when he was driven up in a Rolls Royce bearing the Kabaka's coat of arms above the front bumper. He was accompanied by a Buganda government official whom I had met in Kampala. Expecting a Land Rover I wondered how this car would travel over the murram roads, for I had prepared an itinerary into the worst affected areas 'off the tarmac track'. We set off and I think that the Baganda who saw us drive past must have wondered what two white men were doing in the back of one of the Kabaka's limousines, albeit one of the older ones. I introduced the solicitor to some of the chiefs and showed him some of the worst scenes of arson. We also met a few worried Asian shop owners and I made sure that we drove past my tent and that he saw the Union Jack. I am not sure what he made of his visit, because he made no comments. The Rolls Royce survived as one might expect and I have so far heard no more.

Thus my days out in the bush have been marked with some distracting excitements. The violence has continued and there are a number of cases waiting to be heard. One day a large black Mercedes swept up to the lukiiko hall and Benedicto Kiwanuka, a lawyer and the leader of the mainly Catholic Democratic Party, arrived to defend a man of some means who had been charged with incitement to violence. I was quite apprehensive that Kiwanuka would challenge my conduct of the case, but he fortunately concentrated on challenging the witnesses. I was not convinced and convicted his client. Afterwards I invited him to have some tea at my tent and we had a pleasant and relaxed conversation. He is implacably opposed, as a politician and as a Catholic, to the Buganda Government's policy of frustrating democratic elections. So, once the case had been decided, we were really on the same side.

I am beginning to hear that a few of those convicted and sentenced by me have appealed to the High Court. It will be interesting to hear the results of such action. One woman who cannot appeal, because I only sentenced her to one month's imprisonment, was introduced as one of the Kabaka's singers. The police alleged that her repertoire of songs included one which incited people to violence. She was proud of her role at the Kabaka's court but the court of Butenga sent her to gaol.

I must now finish this letter because Hubert Allen and Robin Palmer are coming for a day's local leave and we are going over to the Sese Islands. The local fishermen at Bukakata run a very good ferry service using their large canoes. We shall land early in the morning and hopefully the ferryman will collect us in the evening.

[1] Speke *Journal of the Discovery of the Source of the Nile* 276
[2] Ibid 268
[3] Lugard *The Rise of our East African Empire* Vol 2, 26
[4] Ibid 23

11: THE RT HON IAIN MACLEOD'S MESSENGER

KAMPALA
10th January 1960

You must be thinking that the ferryman never came to collect us from the Sese Islands six months ago. He did, but time has flown by since then. The islands are extremely beautiful and could become a tourist attraction, but 75 inches of rain a year might discourage the faint-hearted. We saw cattle grazing on open grasslands between the forests but the Basese, the people of the Sese Islands, are predominantly fishermen; their broad shoulders are evidence of hours of paddling in their substantial Sese canoes. These are made from curved planks which are stitched together with banana fibre; more of which is used to effect a tight seal between the planks.

However, the islands and the lake shore have not always been an idyll, certainly not in Winston Churchill's day. "Beyond a blaze of violet, purple, yellow, and crimson blossoms, and an expanse of level green lawns, the great blue lake lies in all its beauty. The hills and islands on the horizon are just beginning to flush to the sunset. . . It must be too good to be true. It *is* too good to be true. One can hardly believe that such an attractive spot can be cursed with malignant attributes. . . Behind its glittering mask Entebbe wears a sinister aspect. These smiling islands which adorn and diversify the scenery of the lake supported a few years ago a large population. Today they are desolate."[1]

The desolation was caused by a form of sleeping sickness, a killing disease spread by a tsetse fly – the glossina palpalis. Other forms of the disease are harmless to man but deadly to cattle. The then Governor, Sir Hesketh Bell, was appalled at the mortality rate; some 200,000 people had died by 1907. He proposed to the Colonial Office that all the people should be removed from the affected areas and resettled at least two miles away from the edge of the lake. In the absence of a reply he put his plan into effect; at a later meeting in London, officials cast doubt about the practicality of his ideas. He then told them that the project was proceeding well and he was informed that the Imperial Treasury would provide funds to complete the operation. He was advised to "go and see the man at the Treasury who deals with grants in aid of Colonies. So I went at once and bearded Chalmers in his den. Contrary to my expectation, he seemed to me to be quite human, and I think I can count on a bit more help in the way of money."[2]

Generally, British financial policy for the Colonies has sought to encourage economic development and self-sufficiency; also, to ensure that all sums raised by taxation are spent on providing services for the people, on development projects and on the budgets of the specialist departments and local governments. For instance, the Protectorate Government's revenue in 1958/59 was just over £20 million and its recurrent expenditure was slightly more. The British Government has assured us that it will provide financial assistance if we cannot maintain government services at acceptable levels. So there is a safety net; paid for by you! You may be surprised that the Colonial Development and Welfare Fund was set up in the early 1940s to provide capital for specific projects. You, like me, might have thought that the British Government would have had other calls on its money during the war. Yet it was right in that many colonies provided troops, particularly for the war in the Far East. Last year the Fund gave the Uganda Government £1.7 million for road building. A start has been made on bituminising the road from Masaka to Mbarara; soon that journey will cease to be a challenge.

However, to return to the 'war' against the boycotters of Butenga. The Governor, having received a Judge's Report, used his powers under the deportation ordinance to deport ten of the movement's leaders to the Northern Province. Then, as we expected, there was a decline in incidents of violence. The boycott reduced trade and a deficit of £500,000 in the revenue budget for 1959/60 is foreseen; so cuts have already been made in grants to the Kabaka's Government. I hauled down my flag and returned to Kampala in early October last year, soon after Graham Moss returned from leave. I am now working in East Mengo for Roy Hiller and living in another small block of flats on the edge of Kololo airstrip – at least I have a good view across Kampala, and the airstrip is no longer used as cross-winds make it too dangerous.

The main event at the end of last year was the publication of the Wild Report in early December. It recommended that there should be direct elections on a common roll to the Legislative Council and an increase in the powers of district councils, with a consequent reduction in those of district commissioners. It rejected as impractical, and possibly counter-productive, any special arrangements for securing the representation of non-Africans in the Legislative Council. The Committee thought that any attempt to do so would harm relationships between the races. Leaving aside the boycott in Buganda, we fortunately enjoy a multi-racial society; except in our clubs. The Protectorate Government has yet to comment in detail on the Report.

While I was away in Masaka for four months the impasse between the British Government and the Buganda Government continued. The latter still boycotts the Legislative Council. The Katikiro of the Kabaka's Government took legal action against the Governor, alleging that he had so altered the composition of the Legislative Council that the Baganda are no longer bound by the 1955 Agreement to send representatives to the Council. The Katikiro's case was dismissed by the East African Court of Appeal last May and an appeal to the Privy Council is now pending. Nevertheless the Secretary of State, Iain Macleod, gave approval for the Governor to meet the Constitutional Committee of the Buganda Lukiiko to discuss amendments to the 1955 Agreement. In these circumstances Macleod visited Kampala in December 1959 and referred to the Wild Report as a pointer to a future constitutional framework for Uganda. In a three-day visit he met the Constitutional Committee and several of the political leaders.

One morning I was instructed to take a letter from the Secretary of State to Milton Obote inviting him to talks. Obote is a northerner from Lango District; in general the Lango people, who are Nilotics like the Acholi, do not have much in common with the Baganda. Obote was said to be staying at an hotel in the Nakivubo market area of Kampala. I drove off at once in my new role as messenger; fortunately I know the area quite well. I told you about the rainstorm there that saved me from a confrontation with rioters one weekend before I went to Masaka. I found the hotel and the Asian owner told me that Obote was upstairs in his room. He opened the letter and his initial response, which I did not hear very clearly, seemed to imply that he would boycott the proposed meeting with the Secretary of State. In fact, he did meet him. It is not surprising that Uganda's politicians have been increasingly irritated by the Baganda on account of their boycotts and their wasteful expenditure on court cases. In a recent speech Obote referred to the 'egg-head' Baganda and I had to read out these words on Radio Uganda news. I was sorely tempted to lay great emphasis on his pejorative remark – I did not do so. In spite of all the differences between the Baganda traditionalists and the non-Baganda nationalist politicians, it became clear that Macleod does not share the Chief Secretary's view that independence is 15 years or more away.

I have been on a number of tours in East Mengo. There is a very senior saza chief known as the Sekibobo of Kyagwe whose headquarters is at Mukono on the railway to Jinja and Kenya. Christopher Kisosonkole is a large, confident and generous man with an independent mind that is rare among his colleagues. He finds no difficulty in encouraging young assistant residents to come and see the progress being made in his saza and I, in my turn, explain our policy for the development of Uganda as a unitary state. I diplomatically refrained from taking this line when the Sekibobo kindly invited me to the ceremonial opening of a school by the Katikiro of Buganda, Michael Kintu. At the lunch afterwards we were, as is the custom, eating chicken and steamed matoke with our fingers. With a chicken bone in his hand Kintu turned to me and said, "Henry VIII used to eat like this!" What could I do, but agree?

The secret of the Sekibobo's independent approach lies in his personality and in the fact that his daughter Damale is the Nabagereka, the Kabaka's official wife. They had met at school at Budu and Damale had later been educated at Sherborne School for Girls in Dorset. Once when I went to Kyagwe the Sekibobo invited me to have a drink on the veranda of his fine house. This is situated on a hill top commanding a wide view of substantial farms stretching towards Lake Victoria. To the east the Lugazi sugar estates cover 11,000 acres, a rare example of plantation agriculture in Uganda. The estate land was bought from out-going British planters who had previously bought land from the original Baganda owners. The Protectorate Government banned such purchases from 1915 onwards at the request of the Buganda Government. The estate and its factory were founded by Nanji Mehta in 1924; there are other Asian-owned sugar estates in Busoga. Sugar production in Uganda has nearly doubled in the last ten years to 81,000 tons, and 13,000 tons were exported last year. The Sekibobo told me that the British planters had formed an association to protect their interests in the period 1908-1929. They planted cocoa, coffee and rubber but the local people were less than willing to become plantation workers and world prices for their crops decreased. Also, at home, opinion was against alienating land in Uganda for non-Ugandans. In the period 1918-1923 the Department of Agriculture and the Uganda Company – owned by Church Missionary Society supporters – persuaded the Protectorate Government that cash crop production of cotton by African smallholders should be encouraged and the British planters discouraged. In any event the latter did not prosper and the fact that a few Asians bought the British planters' land has never been a matter of contention, even at the time of the boycott.

I had first seen the sugar estates from the train when I arrived nearly five years ago and next month I am going on the train to Nairobi. I have volunteered to assist on an Outward Bound expedition, taking some young Ugandans to the top of Mount Kilimanjaro, 19,324 feet. When I applied it seemed to be a great opportunity to escape from the concrete jungle of Kampala to 'the real Africa'. In my urban state of unfitness I am not at all certain that I shall survive the climb and the hazard of mountain sickness!

Meanwhile, I have attended the opening ceremony by the Kabaka of a new session of the Buganda Lukiiko. The Resident and his assistants are traditionally invited to such occasions and we wear our white 'dress' uniforms. The new headquarters of the Buganda Government, known as the Bulange, was recently completed and it is an impressive building set above fine terraces and fountains. It stands at one end of the Buganda version of The Mall, The Kabaka Njagala Road (The Kabaka Wants Me Road) which leads directly to the Kabaka's palace in the Lubiri. The former Bulange was a large traditional mud-and-wattle thatched building within the Lubiri. It is clear to all of us in the Resident's office that it matters little whether the Buganda Government offices are within or without the confines of the Lubiri: in either case little happens without the approval of the Kabaka.

We were advised to arrive at the Bulange in good time. The panelled chamber and the opposed ranks of leather benches reminded me of the House of Commons, but this thought was soon dispelled by the leopard skin covered dais at the far end of the chamber. A finely carved wooden throne was placed on the dais with a smaller chair at a lower level for the Resident. Five large portraits of former Kabakas and one small portrait of The Queen adorned the wall behind the dais. My colleagues and I sat in one of the far corners of the chamber. In the current atmosphere of litigation and heightened political tension the Kabaka's speech was predictably unhelpful. Quite clearly he and his feudal chiefs continue to think that they can resist the trend towards democracy. The Kabaka has a number of friends among the British aristocracy who enjoy visiting his court and are unlikely to give him any objective advice. The ceremony was brief and I and the other assistant residents watched in admiration as Tony Richards, demonstrating the benefit of much practice, proceeded from the council chamber in the wake of the Kabaka's procession. A failure to maintain position by a few inches would have meant that the Resident, like us, would have been the last to leave the building. A cavalcade of cars led by His Highness the Kabaka in his Rolls Royce proceeded to his palace where we enjoyed a reception. In spite of many difficulties, we have friendly relations with several Baganda who work in the Bulange and we met them in the palace. They all speak good English and I rarely need to speak Luganda, although an exchange of greetings is always appreciated. The palace was built in 1924; a long veranda runs across most of the ground floor and the building is crowned with a cupola. Just below this two crossed spears and a shield, the emblem of the Kabaka, are fixed to a wall.

I was delighted to learn at the reception that Ernest Sempebwa, who helped to teach us Luganda at Oxford, is now back here; a casualty of colonial redundancy because there are now no more district officers learning Luganda. I am sure that he must have been disappointed at my feeble efforts to speak his language when we met. He asked me to be his guest that night at a musical celebration in honour of the Kabaka in the grounds of the palace. These grounds are planted as much with bananas as with flowers and

shrubs and thus differ from those at Hampton Court, around which I had escorted Ernest when he came to stay with my parents and me at New Malden. In accepting his return invitation I did not really consider the fact that such events were intended, particularly in this period of intense 'politicking', to concentrate Buganda nationalism and that I would be seen to be playing for 'the opposite team'. Whatever my personal friendships, there was an atmosphere of great excitement as we arrived to take our seats on rickety staging which had been built around an arena over which electric wires and a few lightbulbs had been stretched. Mercifully, as it transpired, there were no lights above the seats. His Highness and his entourage arrived after what seemed an inordinate delay – he tends to equate 'majesty' with a 'make them wait' policy – but he was nevertheless greeted with shouts, the stamping of feet upon the planks supporting our seats and the failure of the lights. I thought that this would be the greatest disaster of the evening, perhaps followed by the collapse of the staging. The Kabaka's drummers were in great form and were evocative of the nationalism and history of Buganda. In the event, neither the lights, which were soon restored, nor the staging presented the greatest dilemma for me.

This came with the announcement of one particular act. One of the Kabaka's personal singers was greeted with rapturous applause and more stamping of many feet upon the staging. To my horror I realised that it was the contentious contralto whom I had imprisoned at the court of Butenga. By chance Ernest and I were sitting behind the Omulamuzi, the Chief Justice of Buganda, and his ample frame provided good cover as I shrank a little in my seat. I felt sure that she could not see me and wondered what would happen to me if our eyes met. I thought that there was little likelihood that this crowd in Kampala would have known of her contretemps with the law in Masaka. I should have realised that her raucous reception meant that the audience knew well that she was yet another 'prison graduate' who had served time in the cause of freedom. Any doubt was dispelled by the next announcement, to the effect that she had recently been released from a British prison in Masaka having been sentenced by a British magistrate at Butenga. I sat even lower in my seat and was so concerned at the possibility of exposure to the lady's wrath that I failed to tell Ernest that I was that magistrate until we were well clear of the celebration! He laughed, but her 'victory', as it was portrayed, and the reception she was given were good indications of the strength of nationalistic feeling in Buganda. It is just as well that I will soon be leaving Kampala for the safety of Mount Kilimanjaro.

[1] Churchill *My African Journey* 90
[2] Bell *Glimpses of a Governor's Life* 164

12: TO BUKEDI,
'THE LAND OF THE NAKED PEOPLE'

BUDAKA
2nd August 1960

Having escaped from the Lubiri without encountering the convicted contralto, Kilimanjaro presented no problems at all! (On the subject of convictions I have now received copies of the High Court judgements on six appeals against my decisions at the court of Butenga. Stephen Kalanzi's appeal against my sentence of seven years imprisonment for arson was dismissed by His Honour Mr Justice Dermot Sheridan. Four other appeals were dismissed, one by the Chief Justice, and another was allowed; the charge had been wrongly framed and I had relied on hearsay.) The day for my departure to Kenya to help on the Outward Bound course followed quickly after that evening of royal entertainment with Ernest Sempebwa. One day in early February I left the Resident's office in Kampala and went down to the railway station to take the train to Nairobi, en route to Loitokitok in Kenya and the challenge of an ascent of 19,324 feet – less the 3,000 or so feet at the base camp. Our walk up Snowdon, 3,560 feet, was but a gentle stroll; especially as we parked the Jaguar at the top of the Llanberis Pass! So I felt somewhat apprehensive as I tried to relax in my seat on the train. I took a book from my case and waited, amidst the usual hullabaloo, for the diesel locomotive to ease out of the station, through the lush countryside of Buganda and across the Nile at the Owen Falls.

Suddenly, a colleague from the Resident's Office came into my compartment. With a degree of drama, heightened by the guard's green flag at the ready, Hugh Cunningham said, "Tony Richards wants to see you now." We both heaved my luggage onto the platform. I felt very foolish as the people on the platform could hardly have thought that I had boarded the wrong train; it was the only departure that afternoon! I next began to wonder what dreadful wrong I must have committed to deserve such a sudden summons. What if the train had left? Would I have been pulled from my compartment by the Sekibobo at Mukono?

All was explained as soon as I entered the Resident's room. "You are posted to Bukedi," he said. "You must leave tomorrow, or at the latest the next day." I know little about the District but I had heard some reports of rioting in January. None of us in Kampala had taken much notice of this news, thinking that we had already experienced more than our fair share of disturbances. Uncharitably, we thought that it was now the turn of our

Eastern Province colleagues to face some riots. After all, I had only returned to Kampala from Masaka four months before. As I sat in the Resident's Office I supposed that my experience at Butenga may have led the authorities in Entebbe to conclude that I was their man for the task of restoring law and order. Then the Resident casually mentioned that some chiefs had been killed and that Frank Gibson, ADC I, had been attacked. Finally, he advised me to travel via Tororo as it was uncertain whether the Terinyi ferry across the Mpologoma River would be operating and whether the road beyond would be closed by roving bands of rioters. At that moment, the prospect of scrambling breathlessly before dawn to the summit of Kilimanjaro appeared positively appealing.

After frantic packing I left Kampala two days later and drove eastwards to Jinja and Tororo and then north to the Bukedi district headquarters at Mbale. My cook, Joseph, and I were more than a little apprehensive – there had been no killings in Masaka. Joseph thought that the Bakedi must be wild unclothed people. I told him that only the Karamojong in the extreme north-east of Uganda still maintained a tradition of nakedness; a condition much frowned upon by the Baganda.

Bukedi – literally in the past 'the land of the naked people' – and other parts of eastern Uganda were not explored in any detail until the British appointed a Muganda, Semei Kakunguru, as their agent, soon after their reluctant declaration of the Protectorate in 1894, and he established his headquarters at Budaka in 1900. Unlike us Kakunguru had taken the direct route towards Bukedi north-east from Jinja, through the centre of Busoga and across the Mpologoma River at Terinyi. Sixty years later Joseph and I eventually arrived at Mbale, the headquarters of both Bukedi and Bugisu Districts, via the longer route using excellent tarmac roads. The town is sited close to the foothills of Mount Elgon, an extinct volcano of 14,178 feet. I reported to Ron Roper, the District Commissioner of Bukedi who had been posted to the District only two weeks before the riots began. Although the violence had by then ceased, the DC explained that the Provincial Commissioner, Tom Cox, had called for additional administrators. It was planned that I and two other district officers would be sent to live out in the sazas in order to re-establish the authority of the local government chiefs. I met Tom that evening and stayed with Ron and his wife Terry for two nights. In the morning I was given a further briefing about the riots. They had been linked to complaints about the graduated tax system and the use of violence by some chiefs to enforce payment. Some blame for magnifying the problem was already being laid at the door of a local politician, Balaki Kirya of the Uganda People's Congress. The DC explained that the main problems had arisen in the north of Bukedi and that I would be stationed at Budaka. You may think that this is a real reversal of history; direct rule by me after indirect rule by Kakunguru 60 years ago!

The next day Frank Gibson drove me westwards towards the main scene of all the trouble. I had no idea what to expect. Ron had told me that seven people, including two chiefs, had been killed by the rioters and that four of the latter had been shot by the police. Many chiefs' headquarters had been destroyed or damaged. In the car Frank related that the riots had been preceded in early January by threatening demands that the DC and the Secretary-General of the Bukedi Local Government should attend protest meetings in Bunyoli. A letter warned them that if there was any delay, "you will find that some people have already been killed." The DC, who met with a crowd of some 6,500 people armed with sticks and pangas, announced an inquiry into the tax assessments. This was greeted with wild excitement and cheers; the people joyfully escorted his car as he left. Nevertheless disturbances broke out on 16th January and lasted until 21st January. Frank described how he had gone to Bulangira accompanied by a police riot squad. The saza chief of Budaka had to be rescued from his headquarters where some 6,000 angry people had gathered. Nearby a crowd of several hundred people attacked the police and chased and struck Frank. Fortunately his injuries were only superficial, but during the fracas the police opened fire and one man died from his injuries. There were further outbreaks of violence; often the crowds numbered some 2,000 people. On 18th January the whole of Bukedi District was declared to be a disturbed area under Section 62(1) of the police ordinance. On that day the PC called for a company of The King's African Rifles. Later two further companies were requested and on 20th January a reserve battalion was put on alert in Kenya. But the situation improved by 21st January and the last of the KAR askaris were withdrawn on 25th January. As Frank recounted these events we travelled through the flat countryside. I had been so lucky to begin my service in Ankole, a land of rolling hills and mountains. Here we were hemmed in by endless banana shambas and plots of cotton, groundnuts, sorghum and, in places, coffee. Only when we looked back eastwards to Mbale were we rewarded with the magnificence of Mount Elgon. I remarked upon the quality of the murram road and Frank explained that the Bukedi Local Government had bought their own road grading machines. He added that the chiefs raise large amounts in taxes, as many of the farmers are comparatively wealthy from sales of produce. Taxes are assessed by the chiefs on the basis of an individual's income from the sale of cotton and coffee, and on the numbers of his cattle, sheep and goats. Additionally each chief has to fulfil a quota.

I forbore to question how a system of assessment according to individual wealth could be compatible with meeting an overall target.

After 17 miles we approached Budaka and I wondered about the condition of the saza chief's house. Would it still have a roof? In Ankole, chiefs' houses were fairly humble dwellings roofed with corrugated iron. I was totally unprepared for the first sight of my new home. At the end of a drive I saw a large white imposing bungalow, roofed with tiles of a colour that is common in Provence. But the most startling feature was the front veranda with three open arches. To each side gabled wings ran back to create a courtyard in the centre where the goats had been kept. An army of prisoners from the nearby gaol were busy cleaning up! To one side local government builders were constructing a raised concrete plinth for an old oil drum with space below for a fire. It is of a height which enables a piped supply of hot water to run by gravity to a newly installed bath in one of the smaller rooms. The cold water is carried from a nearby bore-hole by hand, and poured into the oil drum. There is electricity and the usual pit latrine, some 50 yards away at the back of the house.

On 8th February I took up residence at Budaka and another officer, Bill Clarence, moved into a house at Pallisa to the north. We are being supervised by Basil Branchflower, who arrived in Uganda in 1952. He and I share the house here. He is responsible for Bunyoli to the south as well as for co-ordinating our efforts. One of our first acts, on the instruction of the DC, was to fly the Union Jack from a flagpole in the centre of a circular flower bed in front of our veranda. As we began to drive around the saza we were both shocked by the amount of wilful damage to buildings. All the records had been torn up and scattered around the compounds at many chiefs' headquarters. For the next three months or so we were very busy organising repairs to the buildings, training new chiefs and, by our presence, encouraging the restoration of law and order. This precious commodity, undervalued when part of the everyday pattern of life, is not easily re-established. We were helped by the appointment of a Commission of Inquiry which had been quickly set up by Sir Charles Hartwell, the acting Governor, on 3rd February. It was headed by Mr Justice Bennett and he heard evidence from 180 people: officials, chiefs, politicians, teachers, priests, traders and farmers. Slowly the work of the local government resumed, although it was some time before some of the chiefs concluded that it was safe to sleep in the same place every night. A small Uganda police post was established half a mile away and we were soon thoughtless for our own security as we drove, walked and even cycled around our respective sazas. Occasionally there were alarms. A night of drumming might have presaged a return to rioting and

Basil and I debated whether to investigate. As the noise grew no louder or nearer, we decided that nothing too terrible was afoot. We were told in the morning that there had been a party to celebrate the birth of twins, for whose well-being certain celebrations were deemed necessary. It is a great honour for the father. He is accorded the title 'ssalongo' – the mother is taken for granted!

We received the Commission of Inquiry's Report in early April. The Commission found that the responsibility for "the deaths and damage which we have described must be laid at Mr. Kirya's door."[1] I think that you may find Mr Justice Bennett's conclusion of some interest; it highlights the problems which we face in introducing democratic government here:

> The disturbances in Bukedi had a singularity for there had been an attempt at close identification, through the processes of election, of those in authority and those subject to the authority who came into conflict. Even more remarkable was that the franchise was given to taxpayers only and it was on taxation that the difficulties arose. The attempt was obviously a failure and we conclude that neither the enfranchised nor the elected have yet any proper appreciation that "democracy" does not solve anything by its own inherent qualities. On the part of the elected, we found ambitions beyond fulfilment allied to small executive capacity; we found them to be supported by Administrative Officers bureaucratically concerned with efficiency and material progress. On the part of the electors generally we found no understanding whatsoever. To this disjunction was applied the artifice of unskilled politicians intent on gaining party advantage and who, certainly if their claims to discernment are valid, not only knew and accepted the dangers of their gambit but, we believe, deliberately and successfully played for disorder.[2]

I expect you will notice the criticism of the administration, "bureaucratically concerned with efficiency and material progress." Attention is drawn elsewhere in the Report to the infrequency of touring by the DC and his ADCs. But the judge added that "restoration of order fell to the forces of the Protectorate Government and, with the most minor exceptions, we find their officers performed in an exemplary way."[3] Unsurprisingly the Commission recommended the abolition of the quota system and 'sentenced' my colleagues and me to one year's further service by recommending that "for a period of (say) twelve months officers be retained for duty constantly in the sazas and that they should be without offices to ensure that they do not complain of being tied to routine."[4] Well, I am certainly not aware of any routine in this sort of work.

The publication of the Report was eagerly awaited by the people. Kirya had been banished from Bukedi for six months and we expected that the abolition of the quota and a greater involvement of district councillors in the tax assessment process would be welcomed. However, there was a need to raise funds for the repair of local government property and it was decided to announce a compulsory levy, which would have to be paid by all taxpayers, at the same time as the announcement of the Commission's findings.

It fell to me to hold meetings in all the seven gombololas in Budaka saza on one day. With a minimal police presence, an inspector and six men, I started early and large crowds assembled wherever I went. As predicted the end of the quota produced cheers; but the announcement of the levy caused uproar. The crowds seethed with indignation, anger and fist waving. The police kept a discreet distance from these meetings; a larger number might have been deemed provocative. This number might not have saved my skin! However, in the event there was no violence. At the end of the day I was quite exhausted, but in the evening Basil and I drove round a large part of north Bukedi, visiting Iki Iki, Puti Puti and Goli Goli, amongst other places. Fortunately we found that all was well. Then the time came for people to present themselves at the local chiefs' headquarters to pay the levy; on the first day I sat with the chiefs and slowly the taxpayers arrived and paid for the damage with muted protests.

All of this has been possible because I continue to enjoy a good relationship with the newly promoted saza chief, Yosamu Manye Muswaane. He lives nearby and although I am sure that he would like to move into this house, he seems content with the present arrangement. Together we have selected a number of new and well-educated gombolola chiefs. It falls to my lot to train them. So life was by then returning to normal. The only cloud on the horizon was the inevitable return of Balaki Kirya at the end of his six months' 'exile'. Our apprehension was unnecessary. Although large numbers of people turned out for his first meeting here at Budaka, he was fairly moderate in his demands; except when he called for my removal from the saza chief's house. "That white man must go, why should he fly the Union Jack at our chief's house?" There were overtones, not of his earlier pre-riot rhetoric, but of his campaign for election to the Legislative Council. You may be interested to read his address to the electors:

UGANDA NATIONAL CONGRESS
for INDEPENDENCE and JUSTICE

Bukedi awake, Bukedi awake, elect BALAKI KIRYA,
BALAKI KIRYA, Symbol BANANA. A very bold man
and an expert in debating. For points as these:

1. Multi-racialism in Legco.
2. Immediate Independence for Uganda.
3. Land is our mother, not to be played about with by foreigners.
4. Schools, higher education, industries, hospitals, prisons and trade all to be dealt with vigorously.
5. Increase in cash crops in Uganda for increasing wealth.
6. To abolish the habit of disunity in Uganda. Creation of tribal co-operation among Uganda tribes when only one person is required.

HE IS FULLY PREPARED TO FIGHT SUCH THINGS AND ANY THAT HAS NOT BEEN MENTIONED, BETTER TO DIE THAN TO BE CONQUERED.[5]

After the meeting I asked Balaki Kirya to come to tea with me the next day. He did not complain of my continued presence, or of the larger brand new Union Jack which I hoisted before his arrival. You will probably feel that I was provocative! Maybe. We had a friendly talk about my reasons for working in the Colonial Service and about my view of the future of Uganda as an independent and unitary state. When he drove away I thought of the list in the Report of those who had died and the amount of damage done by the rioters. Two were gombolola chiefs who were beaten to death with sticks; one had first shot a rioter. Damage to buildings is likely to total £280,000.

All of this is, of course, as nothing compared to the recent troubles in the Belgian Congo following the precipitate decision by the Belgian Government to give the Congolese their independence. There was a danger of serious

The new flag flown at the saza chief's house to welcome Balaki Kirya to tea.

disorders and the Uganda Government moved police and army reinforcements to the border. In the event it was only necessary to organise reception and travel facilities for about 4,000 Belgian refugees on their way home to Belgium through Uganda. This is not a good augury for the future but it seems that the Belgians had only made minimal preparations for independence, having previously ruled with a heavy hand. We heard details of this exodus from friends when we invited them to stay for a weekend; some came from Kampala. We are always keen to convince them that living 'out in the bush' need not be uncivilised, illustrating this by offering them a choice of seven different marmalades at breakfast!

Sometimes Basil and I meet up with Bill Clarence in Mbale, where the club is usually full of mainly sedentary townsfolk. There I met Jimmy Fleming, never one to be described as sedentary. He is the Provincial Courts Adviser and, with two or three other extra magistrates, is engaged in hearing cases of alleged rioting; nearly 2,000 people were arrested. During the disturbances Jimmy was asked by Brian Hodges, the District Commissioner Bugisu, to assist the KAR in an operation to pursue some rioters who had been causing trouble on Nkokonjeru, a promontory 7,700 feet high which overlooks Mbale. It is part of the foothills of Mount Elgon. Jimmy met up with a KAR platoon which had descended from the mountains after an unsuccessful patrol. Then an old man came down and reported that there was fighting on or near the top of Nkokonjeru. Jimmy told the effendi (sergeant major) in charge of the platoon, "You must do something." The soldiers were tired and hungry but Jimmy insisted that they should pursue the rioters. The way up was no more than a goat track, the night was dark, the wind rose and heavy rain fell. The effendi, a large man of great bulk but uncertain experience said to Jimmy, "I want you to take charge." Probably Jimmy's army training (in

The Black Watch) was evident to the effendi, but Jimmy declined. The effendi insisted and added, "I'll be your number two." Inevitably Jimmy then led the way with the effendi at the rear. The soldiers asked Jimmy at one point, as they came upon a party of rioters, "Shall we fix bayonets?" Fearful of a massacre, Jimmy refused their request and had to restrain the KAR as they set upon the rioters. But one rioter was felled when a large Acholi soldier swung his rifle butt in a full circle upon the poor man's skull. However, the rioter quickly stood up and shook his head. Later, with the prisoners tied in a line with banana tree fibres, the party descended by a much longer and easier route. Jimmy took leave of the effendi, Idi Amin, and his platoon.

Whilst Jimmy was up the mountain his wife Rosemary helped at the police station at Mbale, noting down messages and reports coming in on the radio. She and many others were kind to us and in return for their hospitality Basil, Bill and I organised a ball at Budaka on April Fool's Day, first sending out invitations from the three of us.

The Collectors of North Bukedi
request the pleasure of the company of

....

at the Ball to be held on Friday
1st April, 1960, at Mile Seventeen, in
Commemoration of the Feast Day of
their Patron Saint.

8 p.m.   *R.S.V.P.*
Black Tie.   *P.O. Box 132, Mbale.*

I should explain that in the early days of our rule some officials were known as 'collectors', as in India, where the title was first used. Taxation there, as here, was a necessary prerequisite for progress. We were able to be precise about the address because I, aided by two prisoners, had moved the mile stone some 50 yards to a site at the head of the drive to our house! The ball was a great success, but I was feeling ill as a result of an accident earlier in the day. I had climbed a short ladder to fit a new bulb in an exterior light on the front of the house and was disconcerted when a wasp came between my eye and my glasses. I knocked the wasp, my glasses and myself off the ladder and fell backwards into a bush with half-inch thorns. I was a sorry sight when I walked into the local medical post. The orderly could not quite understand my explanation, but he cut away my shirt and carefully removed some 20 long thorns from my sore, punctured and now scarred back. Next day I was in hospital with a high temperature.

So, in one way and another, we have our relaxations. I have been fishing for trout with Jimmy at Kapchorwa on the northern slope of Mount Elgon. At other times Bill, Basil and I have been duck shooting at Lake Lemwa near Pallisa. In the evenings I sometimes wander through the fields around Budaka looking for guinea fowl for the pot with the aid of my cheap Spanish shotgun.

Archie Dunbar recruits the porters for our three-day climb on Mount Elgon.

Our agriculture officer, Archie Dunbar, asked me some while ago to join him and the Dean of Pembroke College, Cambridge, on a short expedition up Mount Elgon. Archie was at Pembroke and the Rev Meredith Dewey enjoys visits to his former students in the sunnier parts of the world. At its base Elgon has a diameter of about 50 miles and its crater is some five miles wide. Since its explosive formation about 24 million years ago, there has been extensive erosion and some experts believe that originally it may have been the highest mountain in Africa. Now it is eighth on the list. We set out from the road head above Bumagabula where we recruited a few porters. We were soon climbing through cultivated areas into woodland and eventually onto open heath. Our aim was to reach a hut at 10,600 feet. This was built by the Mountain Club of Uganda and was a comfortable staging post for our climb the next day up to the present edge of the crater. We awoke to find frost on the ground and continued to walk past rock basin lakes formed in a period of glaciation. We then found a considerable change in the vegetation; giant groundsel and lobelia grow to a height of some 15 feet – a phenomenon known to botanists as gigantism. This is attributed to heavy rainfall and, presumably, warm temperatures. We had a limited amount of time to enjoy the views across Bukedi to the west, extending as far as Lake Kyoga. To the east we looked across the vast crater and to the north we could see Mount Kadam, 10,067 feet, in Karamoja. It has a second local name, Debasien; I hope to climb it one day.

.ock basin lake on the igher slopes of .Aount Elgon.

Basil is leaving shortly for a new post in the Secretariat which will involve liaison with the police special branch. Bill and I are due to continue our work as latter-day collectors. New chiefs, improved assessments, the repair of damage and the levy are all contributing to the restoration of law and order. We have recently been given two new tasks. The first, as assistant returning officers, is to oversee the registration of voters prior to new elections to the Legislative Council. This work is due to be completed by the end of this month. The second involves the review of claims for compensation made by individuals whose property was damaged in the riots. First on the list was the claim for the cost of a signet ring, lost by Paddy Erskine, Superintendent of Police. He had broken the ring in the course of restraining a rioter by a blow to his chin. Other claims tended towards exaggeration. Could an elderly descendant of Kakunguru really have had 30 suits in his small house?

Finally, I must confess to a recent wanton act of vandalism. We have improved the grounds around this house, principally by planting an avenue of jacaranda and bougainvillea along the drive in honour of the wedding of Her Royal Highness The Princess Margaret and Antony Armstrong-Jones. I decided one evening to uproot a small withered tree set to one side of the drive. It looked untidy, it had to go and I did not give it a second thought as

Yosamu Muswaane helps Basil and me to plant a new mutuba tree to placate the local Baganda.

I consigned it to the rubbish dump. I enjoy working in the grounds of 'our' property. The local Bakedi were quite astonished when I converted an old water tank into a chicken house and when I cut the hedges on a hot day with my shirt off – half a Mukedi (a person from Bukedi)! They have never seen white men working before! But the removal of the tree had its repercussions. The next day Yosamu arrived while we were having breakfast and demanded to know what had happened to the tree. I showed him the remains and he explained that the tree, a mutuba, had been planted by His Highness the Kabaka on a visit to Budaka two or three years ago. He had received complaints from some local Baganda who were extremely angry. That evening we heard on the news that a close relative of the Kabaka had died suddenly. Then Yosamu arrived with a replacement mutuba tree of a similar height. He, Basil and I planted it and constructed a traditional fence around it. All's well that ends well. The next day I became a little agitated when I saw a man standing on the road staring across at the tree. Was he the first of many protesters? No, he was a special branch policeman, sent to see that there was no more trouble. Basil claims that the man's oversight of our well-being is nothing to do with his new work!

1   Bennett *Report of the Commission of Inquiry into Disturbances in the Eastern Province* 58
2   Ibid 58
3   Ibid 59
4   Ibid 37
5   Ibid 92

13: ELECTIONS AND THE RELATIONSHIP COMMISSION

TORORO
30th June 1961

I think I mentioned that after the riots Mr Justice Bennett had suggested that my colleagues and I should remain en poste in the sazas for "a period of (say) a year." In the event Basil Branchflower was posted in August last year to the Secretariat in Entebbe. He is now working with the police special branch. I remained on my own in Budaka until November when I was posted here to Tororo in the same district. In my last weeks in the saza, Basil came to stay and introduced me to his girlfriend, Joanna. She works in Kampala as a secretary for the Uganda Electricity Board.

view of Mount lgon from the ADC's ouse at Tororo in the irly morning.

Now, as ADC Tororo, I have 'command' of the southern half of Bukedi. I have an assistant, Peter Hunt, one of the few married young district officers. He and Antonia arrived in Uganda in 1958. My large bungalow faces north down the golf course with a magnificent view of Mount Elgon, 25 miles away. You will be pleased to know that the first tee is in my garden! Tororo is a sizeable town on the main road from Kampala to Kenya and it is also on the railway. It is easily seen from many miles across the plains of the Eastern Province because the Rock of Tororo, an eroded volcanic plug, stands several hundred feet high above the edge of the golf course – and my garden. There are cement and asbestos factories nearby. More than 150 Europeans and some 800 Asians live in or around Tororo. It is not surprising that I am more aware of events in the rest of the country than I was at Budaka.

I was sorry to leave but it was clearly time to hand over to Yosamu. He and his gombolola chiefs presented me with a three-legged stool, carved out of a tree trunk, and a double-bladed spear, saying "This will protect your house against all attackers." We had all got to know each other quite well and I was determined to discover my nickname. The Bakedi, like many Africans, "often show a remarkable perception of the characters of white men, officials and others, by the nicknames they give them. English family names are usually incomprehensible to them and they fasten on some personal peculiarity which would be easily recognised by anyone who met them. Thus one would be Master Longlegs, another might be Master Hooknose, and even by indications of his character. I heard of one case where an Assistant District Commissioner was known to the natives as *Bwana Sahani Moja*, meaning Master One Plate. This, I was told, was due to his marked reluctance to entertain guests."[1] None of the chiefs was easily persuaded to divulge my nickname but, after a beer or two, Yosamu said, "We call you Smiling Teeth." No doubt you could think of several worse names!

Following the publication of the Wild Report, Sir Frederick Crawford announced last year that the Secretary of State had agreed that the Legislative Council should have an elected majority and that direct elections should be held on a common roll, with no specific safeguards for minorities. This decision mainly affects the Asian community, most of whom recognise that setting up safeguards may be counter-productive and eventually ineffective. Their strength lies in their vital, but not exclusive, role in commercial and industrial development.

When I wrote to you last August the administration was preoccupied with the registration of voters in 82 constituencies across the country. At the end of this process 1.3 million men and women were listed. This number is much less than it should be and, once again, a boycott in Buganda has caused difficulties. The Kabaka's Government persuaded most of the Baganda to ignore the registration process and there was some intimidation of those who wished to exercise their political rights. In the event only 35,000 people registered in Buganda, out of an estimated 800,000 eligible voters. As I told you in my last letter, the Katikiro has challenged the requirement in the 1955 Agreement that Buganda should be represented in the Legislative Council. His appeal to the Privy Council was dismissed in November last year.

Meanwhile the Secretary of State had agreed to receive the Kabaka and a delegation from the Buganda Lukiiko but their talks were fruitless: the Baganda wanted an assurance of autonomy in an independent Uganda. In

September last year the Secretary of State opened the new parliamentary building in Kampala and announced the terms of reference of a Relationships Commission which will be asked to make recommendations on the best form of government for Uganda. The Kabaka's Government boycotted the opening ceremony and on 8th October the Lukiiko addressed a memorandum to Her Majesty The Queen announcing its intention of abrogating the Agreement and seceding from Uganda on 31st December.

So this year did not start well, but the elections took place on 24th March. I was appointed to be the returning officer for the South Bukedi constituency. The supervisor of elections in Kampala co-ordinated all the arrangements, which were very similar to the procedures used at home. In the weeks beforehand I trained the staff for the polling stations and made arrangements for the delivery of the voting boxes, voting papers and all the paraphernalia of the polling process. When the poll closed the boxes were sealed and transported under safe custody to my office, ready for the count the next day. Each candidate was allowed to have observers and I announced the result from the steps in front of my office in the customary way. The Democratic Party won South Bukedi and obtained a majority over the Uganda People's Congress by 43 seats to 35.

The Governor is the President of the Council of Ministers and of the new Legislative Council. We now have a Speaker, the Hon Sir John Griffin QC, who was formerly the Chief Justice and he, rather than the Governor, normally presides over the Legislative Council. Benedicto Kiwanuka, sometime counsel for the defence at Butenga, is now the Leader of the House. There are eleven Uganda ministers, one of whom is an Asian, and three British-appointed ex-officio ministers in charge of legal affairs, finance, and security and external relations.

Further progress awaits the report of the Relationships Commission. The Chairman is Lord Munster, formerly Parliamentary Under-Secretary of State, Colonial Office. He is assisted by Dr Marshall, City Treasurer of Coventry, and by Dr Wade who specialises in administrative law. They are a high-powered team and have been taking evidence from interested parties throughout the country since they began work in mid-January. They expect to report in June. The Governor has announced that a constitutional conference will be held in London in the autumn and it is thought that Uganda could achieve self-government next year – if all goes well.

You may be surprised at the speed of the projected political development which was greatly accelerated after Iain Macleod's visit last September. It has certainly caused some consternation here and is concentrating the minds of the Baganda in particular. The prospect of independence is upon us: no more and no less than the logical outcome of our policies and efforts. Nevertheless the likely timetable has come as a shock to some, the more so since the Chief Secretary spoke in 1958 of staying for another 15 years. You will no doubt agree that the Commission faces many problems in pointing the way to an independent Uganda. Fortunately, Buganda's threat to secede has had no appreciable effect; the Kabaka was one of the first persons to be interviewed by the Commission. Between the middle of January and the end of March the Commission toured the whole country and talked with 150 people, or groups of people. Unfortunately, Lord Munster was taken ill and returned to England on 8th February, but he is still the Chairman of the Commission.

Thus only Dr Wade and Dr Marshall came to Tororo on Saturday 11th February. In the morning they met the Tororo Town Board and visited the cement factory and Tororo College, which is run by the Catholic Mill Hill Mission. This part of their itinerary had been planned so that Dr Wade, a keen mountaineer, could ascend Mount Elgon. I was asked to make the arrangements and in the time available the ascent was largely by Land Rover through Trans Nzoia district in Kenya. Dr Marshall had no wish to join in this expedition and I therefore took Dr Wade and John Stacpoole of the Colonial Office. He is one of the secretaries to the Commission, the other being Christopher Powell-Cotton, the Provincial Commissioner of the Northern Province, who no doubt ensures that the Commission has access to all the factual information it requires. You might say that his main task is to 'keep them on the rails'. So Dr Wade, Stacpoole and I spent that night at a rest house high up on the Kenyan slopes of the mountain. Around a camp fire we had plenty of time to discuss Uganda and I told Dr Wade about the paper which I submitted to Tony Richards in 1959. In this, you may remember, I stressed the need to encourage latent politicians in Buganda by announcing a clear timetable for self-government. I mentioned that I had proposed, at that time, that there should be an announcement of our intention to grant self-government in 1963 and independence in 1966. We now face the prospect of making all the final preparations for self-government inside one year or so, instead of the five years of preparation and negotiating that are really needed. Dr Wade was interested in the contrasts between our work in the districts and our recent role in Buganda, where most people still toe the line of their feudal chiefs who seek to defend the kabakaship as a means of ensuring their own futures.

The next morning we continued up a track in the Land Rover accompanied by a Kenyan askari. I think the local Kenyan DC wanted to be sure that the Commissioner would come to no harm in his district. Once we began to walk up the final thousand feet or so, we were immediately affected by the change in altitude. Normally this is no problem when walking gradually up a mountain of only 14,000 feet. In spite of his experience Dr Wade found that his legs seemed to be tied together – and so did I! By contrast John Stacpoole, in his somewhat chilly home counties tennis shorts, strode up to the rim without difficulty. Nevertheless we all enjoyed the views and Dr Wade was particularly interested in the vegetation. We made our way down by foot and Land Rover and were back at my house by the evening. They left the next morning to continue their work in Mbale.

Our Kenyan askari escort on the rim of the crater of Mount Elgon which is five miles wide.

A week after the Commission left, Sir Frederick Crawford visited Bukedi. Early on it was suggested that I should stay in an hotel and make my house available for HE. In due course the Government House staff arrived with carpets and silver and set to work on producing canapés for a sundowner, to which all the local great and the good were invited. HE visited the cement factory and a veterinary research centre before leaving the next day to stay at the saza chief's house at Budaka which is still unoccupied, Yosamu preferring to stay in his own house nearby. When I returned to my house I found that the staff had left HE's carpet behind and I delivered it to Budaka, just before he arrived to stay there. His staff were most grateful and shortly afterwards I received a letter from the Aide-de-Camp, Lionel Botcherby, passing on the Governor's thanks for 'letting' him stay at 'my' house!

After all these high level visits I recently went to Kenya with George Sacker, where we enjoyed golf on the highest course in the Empire and a visit to the Nairobi agricultural show. There the livestock were of great interest to George; in my turn I enjoyed the latest tractors and other machinery. I have of late, necessarily, been thinking of my own future. Quite clearly the administration will be one of the first parts of the government machine to be Africanised. I have always had Sir Andrew Cohen's advice in mind. When he talked to Freddie Sheridan and me at some length in Eric Weir's house in Mbarara some years ago he stressed the future need for new skills in an independent Uganda. George is planning to study for the agricultural economics diploma in Oxford, starting in the autumn. I recall that you took this same course five years or so ago, and that you thought rather highly of it. After much discussion with him and other colleagues I have decided to do the same. I am due to go on leave in September and I have received permission to attend the course. I have been granted extra leave for this purpose, so I shall have nine months in England and at the end of that time I hope that I shall have an extra qualification which will be valued here. In this way I should be able to continue my life and work in Uganda. John Cleave, who is one of our original group of six cadets, is planning to do the same. He is now married and the four of us are going to rent Hubert Allen's parents' house at Marston near Oxford – back to the dreaming spires!

Meanwhile, I am planning to join Archie Dunbar and his brother, Sandy, in July on an eight-day trek in the Mountains of the Moon. Sandy works for ICI and has two weeks' holiday so he will hardly be acclimatised. Maybe that does not matter because we shall experience everything from the hottest scrublands to snowy glaciers. I'll write when we are safely down.

---

[1] Bell *Glimpses of a Governor's Life* 193

14: THE MOUNTAINS OF THE MOON

KICHWAMBA
2nd August 1961

Archie Dunbar, Sandy and I have safely returned from an energetic 'lunar' trek around Mount Baker. At 15,988 feet, it is one of the highest peaks in the Ruwenzori; we climbed up through forests and swampy valleys to a land of ice and snow, seeing types of vegetation that seem to have come straight out of wonderland.

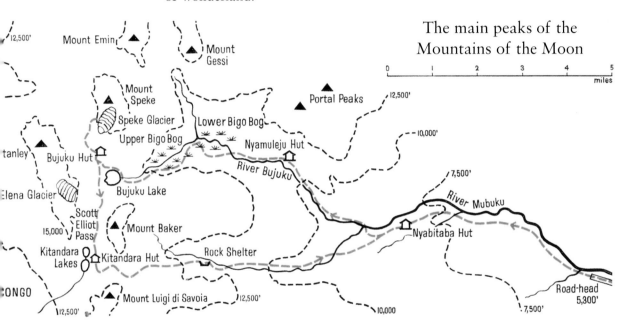

Our circular route around Mount Baker.

The Mountains of the Moon are not one of the earth's great ranges, they extend but 60 miles north to south and 30 miles east to west. They were thrust upwards between two fault lines in the earth's crust some 2 million years ago, in the type of physical formation known to us as a horst – the opposite of a rift valley. There is still some instability in the crust and earthquakes are not uncommon, though usually mild; I felt one or two of them in Mbarara. Although a relatively young range, the rocks of the Ruwenzori are mainly of the Pre-Cambrian era: granitic gneisses, schists and quartzites. Unlike the Virunga mountains in Kigezi and the Congo they are not of volcanic origin, although some small volcanic lakes occur in the nearby Queen Elizabeth National Park.

But this small and young range has acquired a mystique of its own. For years the Greeks speculated about the source of the Nile; tales of its origin in 'fountains' engaged the attention of Herodotus in 450 BC. In AD 150, Ptolemy drew a remarkably accurate map showing the source of the Nile near the Lunae Montes. Others wrote of snowy peaks but most rejected the idea that snow could exist on the equator, which passes below their southern end.

Some 1,700 years passed before Henry Stanley saw the Ruwenzori emerge "from its mantle of clouds and vapours, and showed its groups of peaks and spiny ridges resplendent with shining white snow; the blue beyond was as that of ocean – a purified and spotless translucence. Far to the west, like huge double epaulettes, rose the twin peaks which I had seen in December, 1887, and from the sunk ridge below the easternmost rose sharply the dominating and unsurpassed heights of Ruwenzori proper, a congregation of hoary heads, brilliant in white raiment."[1]

One of Stanley's party, Lt Stairs, climbed through the forests in the foothills before reaching an altitude of 10,677 feet. He calculated that the snowy peaks were some 6,000 feet higher, but was unable to progress further due to the bitter cold of the nights and lack of equipment for his men who complained of fever. Stairs was remarkably accurate because Margherita, the highest peak on Mount Stanley, is 16,794 feet.

Now, 72 years later, we have all the advantages of excellent maps and the opportunity to stay in the huts built by the Mountain Club of Uganda, which I applied to join some three months ago. David Pasteur, as secretary, duly informed me of my election as a full member and supplied details of the huts and routes, together with advice on the recruitment of a guide and porters. When the time came, I left Tororo early in the morning and drove via Kampala to Fort Portal where I met Archie and Sandy. We stocked up with provisions before driving south the next day to the road-head near Bugoye where we met our guide and the porters. The Bakonjo live in the foothills and are well used to carrying loads, using straps made from banana fibre around their foreheads. We had calculated their number according to the weight of our own kit and provisions and also of their food. The club recommend a daily ration for each porter of $1^{1}/_{2}$ lbs maize flour, 5oz of dried or smoked fish, 3oz of beans or groundnuts, together with salt, sugar, tea and cigarettes. The number of porters required is based on each of them carrying a maximum load of 50lbs. We had to calculate the weight of our personal baggage, our provisions and of their food. We agreed the standard pay of Shs 2/50 per day, plus sweater, blanket and an allowance for walking barefoot on snow!

All the loads were eventually sorted evenly onto willing backs and, with our guide leading the way, we moved off at noon through elephant grass which we clearly shared with elephants, although we did not meet any. Our first objective was the club's hut at Nyabitaba, 8,400 feet. This was not so energetic as you might think because we started from about 5,000 feet at the road-head. After a while we emerged through the elephant grass and the path, if path it may be called, followed the Mubuku river before rising steeply above it through the cool rain forest where symphonia trees rise to 90 feet and form a canopy for begonias, balsam and some hibiscus below. We stopped for tea at a point where we could see up and down the Mubuku valley. We were on a ridge and we knew that our hut lay ahead; but each time we thought that we were about to arrive, there was still more of a climb along the narrowing knife-edge. There were many 'false crests' before we reached the hut; sparsely furnished with simple beds, it became our home for the night. Our porters camped nearby under a rock shelter where one of them cooked our supper which we washed down with tea laced with brandy – to keep the chill of the night away.

Next morning we had a sight of the Portal Peaks, bare rocky summits, too low for snow to lie upon them. Then we dropped down towards the Mubuku which we crossed just below its confluence with the Bujuku river, using a swaying suspension bridge of wire and struts, some of which were missing. Then we set out to walk to the Nyamuleju hut at 10,640 feet. Following the valley of the Bujuku we made our way through shrubs and moss before entering the heather forest; the heather in this environment grows to some 20 feet in height. The trunks and branches were weirdly covered in exotic mosses and lichens and we appeared to have entered a green cauldron, topped with mist, for we could hardly see the steep slopes of the valley and side valleys rising from the boggy floor. The day's climb is only just over 2,000 feet but the effort of finding footsteps through the moist and slippery tangle of fallen branches, rocks and mimulopsis made the climb seem much more arduous. Nevertheless we arrived in good time at Nyamuleju, 'the place of the beards'. The mists and clouds, which had lain above us all day, parted as the evening came and to our great joy we suddenly saw high above us the snowy summit of the Mount Stanley plateau and the slopes of Mount Speke. We were at the same altitude as Lt Stairs and the thought that we might be in the middle of these snowy giants in one day's time was awesome. We climbed a rock behind the hut to improve our view and stood transfixed until the sun set. On our third day we learnt at breakfast that the porters had successfully caught several hyraxes, rodent-like animals weighing up to 10 lbs whose ability to run vertically up trees and rock faces is derived from their peculiar toes which, some experts say, indicate that they are distantly related to the elephant – maybe to a pink one!

Our next objective was Lake Bujuku, only some 2,300 feet above us, but the terrain changed from difficult walking to the daunting challenge of

The upper Bigo bog through which we passed with great difficulty.

negotiating the Bigo bogs. As we emerged from the heather forest we found ourselves in a world of giant groundsel and lobelia, some 15-20 feet high, on the impassable slopes of the widening glaciated valley. Our only course was to stay in the valley bottom and traverse the bog, initially by jumping from one giant tuft of grass to another. We became quite skilled, leaping from tuft to tuft some six or seven times before tired legs or ill-judgement brought us down into the muddy bog which came well above our knees. Eventually it seemed easier to plough through this mud rather than to continue these athletic efforts. This was the most arduous part of our journey so far and we were encouraged by the widening views of Mounts Baker, Stanley and Speke around a cirque in which, after one near vertical climb, we saw Lake Bujuku. We knew that we were then within a short distance of the hut and when we arrived we just sat and looked around an amazing amphitheatre. The lobelia and groundsel rose up to meet their limits on the rocky screes which themselves led up to snowy slopes and, on Speke, to a gleaming glacier.

We spent two nights at Lake Bujuku and we were extraordinarily lucky to have perfect weather and blue skies. At each hut there is a visitors book and we read many reports by our predecessors recording bad weather and, sadly, "We have seen nothing of the peaks." We turned in fairly early on our first night; both Archie and Sandy were feeling the effects of altitude and we wanted to be fit for the climb up to the snout of the Speke glacier next day.

In the morning, before breakfast, I had a quick, very quick, dip in a small stream; one of the many in the floor of our amphitheatre. It was amazingly refreshing! We set off up the Stuhlman Pass and at a point where it descends

From one giant tuft of grass to another – or into the bog!

towards the Congo we struck up the steep western flank of Mount Speke. The going was rough, half scree, half rocks and very little vegetation. We reached the glacier; at 14,400 feet it was the highest point of our journey so far. The blue water flowing from the snout was like champagne but the ice itself was remarkably dirty, being full of grit and stones; glaciers are simply giant excavators. We could see a way towards the summit and it was a tempting thought, but we were not equipped for traversing ice, were aware that the weather could change with dramatic speed and that we were two days' fast marching from civilisation and any rescuers. Looking across to Margherita, now only about 2,400 feet above us, we at least felt like mountaineers.

The view of giant groundsel at 14,500 ft with Mount Stanley's snow-capped plateau seen from the Scott Elliot pass.

After our second night at Lake Bujuku we left the amphitheatre via the Scott Elliot Pass. This involved a steep climb up loose scree in which giant groundsel maintained a grip more easily than we did. The pass was covered in snow and lies between Mount Stanley and the nearly vertical flanks of Mount Baker. Our way down the pass was strewn with rocks and our porters ran for their lives as they had witnessed many falls of rock on previous trips. We were spared. We stayed the night in a hut on the shores of Lake Kitandara, famed for its stillness and for acting as a mirror to the golden jagged peaks of Mount Luigi di Savoia at sunset. At other times, as on our visit, it presents a dark and unnervingly sombre stillness.

The next day we climbed up again, this time to the Freshfield Pass. On the way we had superb views of the Coronation glacier and the Elizabeth and Philip peaks nearby, all on the southern end of the Mount Stanley range. Once over the col between Mount Baker and Mount Luigi di Savoia it was to be 'downhill all the way home'. Our last night was spent under a rock shelter with a stream cascading nearby. We completed our circular 'walk' around Mount Baker early the following day when we rejoined the path which led us back to the road-head. We thanked our guide and our porters and paid them their well-earned dues, for certainly we could not have travelled without their cheerful, willing company. In seven days we had seen but two fellow walkers and, as we surveyed the dusty plains of Toro, we felt as though we had been in a different world – but then we had been to the Mountains of the Moon. I can see them now as I finish this letter on the veranda of the Kichwamba Hotel. Tomorrow I shall return to Tororo via Mbarara and will be flying home to Lymington, my parents' new home, in three weeks' time.

Standing near the Speke glacier with the Stanley plateau in the background.

Our last view of the glaciers on the southern end of the Stanley plateau.

[1] Stanley *In Darkest Africa* Vol II, 231

15: SENTENCED TO SERVE IN THE SECRETARIAT

ENTEBBE
15th April 1962

When we met in Oxford before Christmas, I explained that my chances of obtaining a diploma in agricultural economics had ebbed away with the realisation that I would never understand statistics, an integral part of the course and, to me, the equivalent of Chinese algebra! So I returned here in mid-March and, ironically, I have now been sentenced to serve in the Ministry of Agriculture and Animal Industry here in Entebbe. I am getting used to the role of an assistant secretary. Collectively the several ministries are still known as the Secretariat and I have already told many of my friends up country that they must inform me at once if they detect any signs that I may have become infected with 'Entebbeitis': a condition characterised by an addiction to paper, a belief that those in the centre know better than those on the ground, and a creeping paralysis of the powers of decision. But, of course, it is already clear to me that we in Entebbe, having an overview of government action across the Protectorate, are better placed to prescribe policy than those in the districts!

There is a possibility that our office will be moved to Kampala and I stayed initially in the Lake Victoria Hotel, as I did when I first arrived in 1955. As respect requires, I signed the Governor's visitors book on the first evening. Sir Frederick Crawford retired last November. He had the satisfaction of signing an important new Buganda Agreement following a constitutional conference in London last autumn. Our new Governor is Sir Walter Coutts, who was formerly Chief Secretary in Kenya. One day at lunch in the hotel I met two policemen from Kampala who had been sent to smarten up the police guard at Government House. Lady Coutts had not been amused to find the police throwing stones at the mango trees near the guardroom; presumably to check Newton's theory, or maybe to enjoy the fruit and while away the long hot hours! Clearly our new Governor and his wife have not been impressed by such behaviour. One evening I saw them both walking across the golf course towards Lake Victoria; two tall figures deep in conversation and on their own without any form of escort.

I had hopes of being allocated one of the older balconied and bougainvillea be-decked flats with a view of the lake. However, my bachelor housing points have dictated that I must be content with a new and rather sparse ground-floor flat on the road to the airport. Instead of the fine view of Mount Elgon from my lovely house at Tororo, I can now only see a banana shamba in which a shop seems to be a centre for frequent loud beer-drinking parties, just when I try to go to sleep. But the flat is near the office, and as my Triumph Herald has yet to arrive at Mombasa, Tosca and I walk to work twice daily. She stayed with Archie Dunbar while I was in Oxford and she now misses the constant coming and going of visitors in an up-country district headquarters. I dare not tell her that we shall not be going on tour!

I should explain that since I left to go on leave last August there has been a rapid acceleration in an already fast process of political development. You might find this list of recent events helpful in keeping up to date:

December 1959	The Wild Report published.
August 1960	Registration of Voters.
September 1960	Iain Macleod opens the new parliament building and announces the Relationships Commission.
December 1960	The Kingdom of Buganda 'secedes'.
March 1961	The Democratic Party wins the general election. Benedicto Kiwanuka becomes Leader of the House.
June 1961	The Relationships Commission reports.
July 1961	Benedicto Kiwanuka becomes Chief Minister.
September 1961	London constitutional conference.
December 1961	Registration of voters.
March 1962	Self-government. Benedicto Kiwanuka becomes Prime Minister.

You will recall that I helped organise the March 1961 elections which were won by the Democratic Party, largely because the party gained 20 of the 21 Buganda seats in the Legislative Council. I really do think that the Baganda have been their own worst enemies in recent years. By boycotting these elections the Kabaka's Government effectively put a Catholic-dominated government in place. Benedicto Kiwanuka became an increasingly implacable opponent of the Kabaka's Government, which has always been a

Protestant preserve. It is so sad that Uganda's religious wars of the last century cast such long and deeply divisive shadows today.

You will have read something in your newspapers about the London conference which began last September: 48 representatives of the kingdoms and the districts considered the recommendations contained in Lord Munster's report. There are 19 pages of summaries of his recommendations, so it was never going to be a short conference! An important breakthrough was the agreement that the Baganda would at last send members to the proposed National Assembly, either by direct elections or indirectly. In the latter case the Buganda Lukiiko would act as an electoral college.

The reason for this probably lies in the formation last June of a new organisation called Kabaka Yekka, which means 'the Kabaka alone', i.e. the only ruler. This is now playing a major part in Uganda politics although it is not really a political party. It was conceived to maintain the traditions of Buganda and is led by Augustine Kamya, a leading figure in the instigation of the boycott of Asian traders in 1959/60. The Buganda establishment – the Buganda Government and its chiefs – does not attempt to conceal its interest in the movement. I do not know whether the Kabaka and his government are actively supporting Kamya, but it seems almost certain that they might see advantage in such action although they distrust even quasi-politicians. In any event, this organisation has a traditional majority in the Buganda Lukiiko. If the Lukiiko, as may be expected, chooses to elect Buganda's 20 members to the new Assembly indirectly, then the Democratic Party may lose their present majority when pre-independence elections are held later this month.

Kiwanuka's position has lately been further weakened by an electoral alliance between Kabaka Yekka and Milton Obote's Uganda People's Congress. This is thought by most people here to be a marriage of convenience at best and an unholy alliance of opposites at worst. Obote's party is dominated by Nilotic northerners who, it cannot be denied, tend to despise the 'banana-eating' Bantu Baganda. The question is whether this particular alliance can become a coalition that is capable of uniting the country. In desperation Kiwanuka has authorised spectacular increases in coffee prices and in the wages of government workers. Additionally, promises have been given that Africanisation will be accelerated, and separatist movements in parts of the country have been irresponsibly encouraged; all in the pursuit of votes. Amongst his responses Milton Obote has assured the electorate that, when he wins the election, he will see that the Europeans are put to work mending the roads!

The London conference also decided that self-government would be granted to Uganda on 1st March this year. (Kiwanuka has thus been Prime

Minister for only six weeks.) Then, to the general surprise of the conference, Macleod unexpectedly announced at the final session, "Uganda will be independent one year from today", i.e. on the 9th October this year! So the period of self-government is destined to be some seven months only. This is a very much shorter period than the equivalent time allowed in those territories which have already achieved independence.

Incidentally, Russel Barty, who served with me in Mbarara, is now personal assistant to Kiwanuka. Russel tells me that the Prime Minister is prone to make lavish promises on tour when confronted by his people. They have great and, I fear, unrealistic hopes that independence will immediately bring them prosperity – higher prices for their crops and more schools for their children. Russel then has to be the middle man between the Prime Minister's largesse and the harsh reality of, for example, the Ministry of Education's funds in the current budget. Russel has also been involved in planning Uganda's embryonic foreign service. Initially high commissioners will be appointed to the UK and to some Commonwealth countries; also ambassadors to the United Nations and to the United States.

In the light of all these changes, Peter Allen, the Permanent Secretary to the Prime Minister, wrote to all the administrative officers last November. He asked us whether we would stay on after independence or elect to leave under a compensation scheme, probably on the lines of the arrangements made in Tanganyika. He explained that he had had informal discussions at the Colonial Office and with the head of the Resettlement Bureau. The latter had advised him that officers under the age of 35 years were likely to find a new career more easily than those over 40.

I and all my colleagues, certainly those who came out here in the 1950s, have always accepted that our task has been a self-denying ordinance in career terms. Yet it was more than a little shock to receive such a letter during the economics course at Oxford and to be invited to make a choice which might end seven years of varied, responsible and constructive work amongst such generally delightful people – in an amazingly beautiful country. In my reply I emphasised that I would much prefer to remain in Uganda for as long as I might be required and that I was prepared to work for a stable African government, subject to reasonable working and living conditions. The prospect for older staff of having to find new employment is undoubtedly worrying, especially for those with families. Morale may suffer, just at the testing time of handing over our work. The vast majority of expatriate staff will be very sad to leave.

When I decided to abandon the course, I wrote again to Peter Allen at the end of January. I explained my reasons for leaving Oxford and admitted that

I was considering an alternative career in the British Council. I asked, with the greatest misgiving, whether I might be Africanised and whether I would be required to return at the end of my leave in March, only six months before independence. But in so many ways the last thing I wanted was to have my career terminated so abruptly, especially if it meant that I would have no chance to say goodbye to so many friends – and to Tosca. You will not be surprised that I asked to be posted, in the event of my return, to the Western Province, West Nile or Karamoja. In his reply to me John Champion, in the absence of Peter Allen on leave, wrote, "I can say here and now that you will be required to come back on 16th March. I am afraid that we will almost certainly not be able to meet your wishes about your posting when you return; the present intention is that you will go to the Ministry of Agriculture and Animal Industry." So much for the wilds of Karamoja!

Now I am back, office-bound and adjusting to the fact that the Hon Benedicto Kiwanuku is the Prime Minister of a self-governing Uganda. My minister is the Hon BJ Mukasa. He welcomed me to his staff but I doubt that, at my level, I shall see much of him, particularly as pre-independence elections will be held later this month.

There is a real sense of urgency and I find it quite strange that I am not involved in organising the elections once again. Entebbe seems really rather remote from the real action. For my part, under the direction of Brian Hodges, now the Permanent Secretary, I am grappling with the consequences of the coffee price assistance fund, whereby growers were shielded from the worst fluctuations in the world price of coffee. You were right all the time in criticising government intervention in coffee prices. The accumulated funds, in reality the savings of the growers, were diverted by the Protectorate Government in Sir Andrew Cohen's time to fund investment in new industries, such as the Tororo cement factory and Nyanza textiles. I know that you believe that this was premature because the embryonic markets for these new products had then to be shielded from cheaper imports. Nevertheless the expansion of coffee production has been a success. Before our time robusta coffee was grown in the wild and the Baganda cultivated small plots. They used to chew the unripe cherry after steaming and drying it. Arabica coffee was introduced from Nyasaland in 1900 and grows best over 5,000 feet, almost exclusively on the slopes of Mount Elgon. As early as 1932, under the terms of a coffee grading ordinance, African-grown coffee had to be graded by government graders at a licensed factory. Most of these are owned and run by Asians, just one facet of their commercial investment which has helped Uganda to prosper. Others are owned by African co-operatives. There are now nearly half a million acres of African-grown coffee. In 1960, 105,000 tons of processed coffee beans were produced and the growers received an income of £12 million.

Our Minister will, in his life-time, have seen some huge changes. It hardly seems possible to me that Uganda is self-governing. The Prime Minister is determined to win the pre-independence elections later this month. They will be based entirely on universal adult suffrage; there will be no nominated, appointed or ex-officio members in the new Assembly. You may remember that I met Benedicto Kiwanuka in 1959, when he appeared as a defence lawyer at the court of Butenga. There I flew the Union Jack in the Buganda countryside, much to the irritation of the Kabaka. I and some Protectorate police camped out in the bush near Masaka in response to an outbreak of violence and intimidation arising from a boycott of Asian shops. As I wrote at the time, I entertained Kiwanuka to tea outside my tent and we had a very friendly discussion about the future. Then, neither he nor I would have thought it possible that Uganda would be on the verge of independence less than three years thereafter. We both agreed that the resistance of his fellow Baganda to political development was then placing their kingdom at a disadvantage. The Protectorate Government solved the problems of the boycott by firm action, but the Buganda Government threatened to secede in December 1960. Fortunately nothing really happened, the life of the Protectorate could not be so simply changed. And so, here in the Ministry, as we await the elections on 25th April, we see our present work being affected by politics, and you will no doubt be saying that this proves that government interference in prices is never a good policy.

Out of the office I am finding my way round the lake-side golf course, and enjoying the club and the swimming pool. Next weekend I am flying to Nairobi so that I can attend the baptism of my niece, Penelope. I may not have told you that Margaret was posted to Kenya where she met John Ryan in 1956; I gave her away at her wedding at Nanyuki in May 1957. Then I will collect my car from the railway, and drive back across the Rift Valley and the heights of the Kenya highlands around Timboroa Summit. I am glad that I came back, even if I am a pen-pusher!

16: A SUMMONS FROM HIS EXCELLENCY

ENTEBBE
10th June 1962

You probably gathered from my last letter, written as a ministry pen-pusher, that I was not entirely happy in that role.

Now I have some real news. Four weeks ago, Brian Hodges came into my office and told me that I had been appointed Private Secretary to His Excellency the Governor, Sir Walter Coutts. As my Permanent Secretary he was probably upset that he would, so soon, have to start training my successor, but the warmth of his congratulations matched the depth of my surprise and excitement. He then simply told me that I should ring the present Private Secretary, Martin Fleay, and make an appointment to see HE. I had once met Martin on a visit to Karamoja, where he was then the District Commissioner. On that occasion some friends and I climbed 10,000 feet to the top of Mount Debasien. But that day I had no knowledge of the heights which I would have to scale in my new task, only a rapid realisation that Government House was likely to be a hive of activity, with only five months left before independence and the hauling down of the Union Jack. Later that morning, I nervously drove up the hill to Government House, or GH as it is known more briefly. It has commanding views over Entebbe to Lake Victoria and I had been there twice before in 1955. A messenger, whom I now know as Suleimani, came out to conduct me to Martin Fleay's office on the first

The ceremonial entrance to Government House and, to the left, the office wing.

floor of the office wing. From his desk he has a view of the lake, the airport and the main driveway up to the porte-cochère, which forms the ceremonial entrance to Government House. Martin told me that he is going to the Treasury, I think on promotion, but I could not help but feel that he might well have wanted to stay on until independence. However, he ushered me along the corridor to Sir Walter's office, which has the same outlook but the benefit of shade from the gaunt remnants of a very large tree, host to a rampant climber with brilliant orange flowers. The Governor seemed to tower above his desk. His warm greeting was followed by a searching question: "How do you think you will like this work?"

As I knew little of what it might involve, beyond perhaps organising HE's papers, drafting letters and co-ordinating programmes of events and visitors, I just managed to mumble that I considered it an honour to be asked to work for him. He soon put me at my ease with his warm smile, and explained that he wanted to make changes to the organisation of Government House, not just to the running of his Office. This was more than a surprise as I assumed that there were plenty of people to look after the Household. I already knew Lionel Botcherby, the Aide-de-Camp, who had accompanied Sir Frederick Crawford to Tororo when I was stationed there. Sir Walter said that he wanted me to be in overall charge of both the Household and his Office and he suggested that I might need to hold a weekly meeting in order to improve co-ordination. HE expressed concern that independence and a Royal Visit would involve a very great increase in work and mentioned that he wanted to build a good relationship with the Prime Minister, Milton Obote, and his Cabinet. The Prime Minister is already a regular visitor to Government House and Sir Walter plans to invite the PM and his ministers to informal dinners with the leaders of the various communities and churches.

Here I should tell you that the coalition of Obote's Uganda Peoples' Congress and the Kabaka Yekka Movement had won the election at the end of April, as I predicted in my last letter. Last October the London conference had determined that the election should be in April, but I have seen from papers here that Benedicto Kiwanuka and his Cabinet delayed the issue of the writs, seeking more time to consolidate their political strength outside Buganda. In order to play for time Kiwanuka arranged for the three rulers of the western kingdoms, Toro, Ankole and Bunyoro, together with the Kyabazinga of Busoga, a would-be king, to travel to London to press their case that their kingdoms, like Buganda, should be given federal status. These tactics were overcome by an amending Order in Council, which empowered the Governor to issue the writs without the Cabinet's advice. Now Benedicto Kiwanuka is the Leader of the Opposition.

I told the Governor that I had briefly met Obote when I was in the Resident's Office in Kampala and knew one of his principal lieutenants, Balaki Kirya; almost too well! Sir Walter indicated that he knew of my experiences in Masaka and Bukedi. I wonder whether his appointment of me, surprisingly without any preliminary interview, indicates that he wants someone with experience of trouble-shooting?

I had the rest of that day and the next to understudy Martin Fleay, although he was partly pre-occupied in moving out of his house. This is in the grounds close to the office wing and when he showed me round I was delighted to find that it was a typical up-country style bungalow, with a green painted corrugated-iron roof, lofty rooms but, alas, no veranda. Not that I can expect to have much time to admire the views across the gardens, the tennis court and the lake.

Between my office and HE's office, there is a small room for Margaret Luke, HE's personal secretary. He dictates notes of all his conversations and meetings so I am not normally required to act as a note-taker. This is just as well as it would preclude my attending to many other pressing tasks. Margaret brings all her work on letters and notes to me to see and, after reading them, I take them in to the Governor for his approval and signature.

At the end of my first day on my own I came down the stairs and met Lady Coutts. A tall, slim and gracious woman with an air of authority, she asked me when I would be moving into my house. She is known to her friends as 'Bones', a nickname arising from her height and slight build. She enquired whether she should attend my projected weekly meetings of all the senior Government House staff. I replied that I did not think that she need do so, adding that her secretary, Pam Parker, would be present together with Margaret Luke, Lionel Botcherby, the housekeeper and the accountant, Cosmo de Souza. He is a Goan and his people have an aptitude for figures and a high reputation for their honesty and reliability. They fill many of the financial posts in the Protectorate Government. Pam is very experienced, having been at GH for over three years; she first came for two weeks to help out in Lady Crawford's office. I have the impression that Lady Coutts may have persuaded Sir Walter that the Household had not been working as well as that at GH Nairobi, where on occasions Sir Walter had been acting Governor. Lionel told me later that Lady Coutts, on hearing of my appointment, had asked whether I had signed the visitors book. Fortunately I had done so and I looked through the older books to find my initial entry in 1955. There, six names above mine, was written 'WF Coutts, Nairobi'.

In due course I moved from the airport road flat to my new house and my cook, Paulo, is very impressed to find himself living alongside the Governor's retinue of servants, not to mention the Governor!

After just four weeks the extent of the work involved in bringing Uganda to independence is becoming clear. Sir Walter informed me during my first week that there would be another constitutional conference in London later this month. Apparently when Iain Macleod announced last October that "Uganda will be independent one year from today" there was a great hush and he turned to Sir Walter, who was in attendance as the Governor designate, and said, "OK Wally?" A Ugandan sitting next to Sir Walter commented softly, "That would be quite impossible." It was easy for Macleod to say this as he left the Colonial Office the next day to become Leader of the House. He advised his successor, Reginald Maudling, that "Uganda is all wrapped up." But Sir Walter told me that it was abundantly obvious to him, in spite of being a newcomer to the Uganda scene, that too many problems had been swept under the carpet. Certainly Buganda had moved towards accepting a united Uganda, but the relationship of the kingdoms to the central government had not been settled in any detail. Sir Walter said that he had insisted on seeing Maudling after the conference and, to the surprise of the new Secretary of State and his officials, pointed out that a second constitutional conference would be required.

During this period of self-government the Governor is responsible for foreign affairs and defence as well as for overseeing the political progress towards independence. Formerly, some of this work fell on the shoulders of the Chief Secretary but that post was abolished when Benedicto Kiwanuka became Chief Minister prior to the introduction of self-government. A Deputy Governor has been appointed. He is the Hon Barry Cartland and he has his own small staff. They work in a new modern office in the woods just outside the grounds of GH. This means that I shall not be closely involved in the detail of the work on the constitution. The scale of the tasks facing the Deputy Governor and the Attorney General is illustrated by the fact that the Legislative Council had to pass 26 ordinances in 18 days before the introduction of internal self-government.

Some people here question how independence can be achieved by a government of contradictions, a strange blend of radicals and traditionalists. But I am glad to be able to tell you that the Prime Minster, although he may have had some hard bargaining with his new found Kabaka Yekka supporters, has achieved an acceptable balance in the distribution of ministerial portfolios. Five of these are held by members of Kabaka Yekka, including finance, education and health. Mr JT Simpson, the Chairman of the Uganda Development Corporation, is the Minister of Economic Affairs, an appointment designed undoubtedly to reassure the commercial community and foreign investors. But you may note that Obote has shrewdly placed his own supporters in the ministries responsible for police, justice, information and local government – the essential levers of power.

I first met the Prime Minister in my new role very soon after I began work here. When I escorted him into GH there was no mention that my next employment would be on the roads! I am sure that his electioneering talk had only been aimed at the electorate. The occasion was a lunch in honour of the visiting Deputy Prime Minister of Tanganyika. The Governor asked me to attend, although the Private Secretary is not usually expected to be at such functions. It is the role of the Aide-de-Camp to receive guests, introduce them to HE and Lady Coutts, generally assist in placing people at their ease, indicate the seating plan, which he will have drawn up, and ensure that the occasion flows smoothly. My presence added little to the success of this lunch. The conversation was really rather limited and I don't think that I was of any assistance.

After lunch, when HE came from the first floor corridor in the main part of GH into my office, he remarked, "That was a very sticky luncheon." I thought that my career would be very short indeed. Even Lionel Botcherby, who usually has plenty of social conversation, was unable to contribute. As Aide-de-Camp he lives in GH and is always on duty at any functions, and at lunch and dinner whether or not there are any guests. He therefore has the opportunity and a very important task to keep me informed of the Governor's requirements and comments.

Lionel, who came out to Uganda to join the police, can be quite autocratic with the staff and about ten days after I arrived here there was a crisis for which he was largely responsible. One of our exports, alongside democracy, is the encouragement of trade unions. But I doubt if anyone in the Ministry of Social Development and Labour anticipated that the GH drivers would threaten to go on strike as a protest against HE's Aide-de-Camp! The thought that the Rolls Royce landaulette, purchased second-hand for Her Majesty The Queen Mother's visit in 1959, the Austin Princess and an ageing Humber limousine, together with a large new Pontiac for up-country travel, a Humber Super Snipe and a Land Rover could all be immobile was simply unacceptable. I held discussions with Pip Coutts, Sir Walter's brother, who was head of the Nsamizi Training Centre, and who is now the Permanent Secretary of that Ministry. The ring leader was posted back to the Ministry of Works whence he had come, normal work was resumed and the wheels kept turning. I shall have to make sure that Lionel changes his ways. He is the same age as I am, although he has much longer experience here; but I have to be in control, if the left hand is to know what the right hand is doing.

Occasionally I have to go to Kampala, where the Governor has a small lodge at Makindye, on a hill just outside the city. I am usually driven in the Humber Super Snipe, with rather more room than in my own Triumph Herald. Sir Frederick Crawford bought this for his up-country journeys, but the long legs of Sir Walter and Lady Coutts are now better accommodated in the Pontiac. Its longer wheelbase rides over corrugated murram roads much more smoothly. At the moment, however, there is no time for touring as there is so much to do here in Entebbe and in Kampala.

The Kabaka sometimes visits the Governor. Once he drove himself from Kampala in a brand new Rolls Royce; he had bought it and a new Bentley at the same time! His garage includes a number of stately older Rolls Royces. When he comes I welcome him at the main entrance and escort him to Sir Walter's office. He is invariably extremely polite; I told you he was a Cambridge graduate and a Guards officer. Our brief conversations do not touch on the once contentious issue of my flying the Union Jack in his Kingdom at Butenga near Masaka.

One morning recently, the Governor, who is also Commander-in-Chief of Uganda, received two Ugandan soldiers to whom he presented commissions as second lieutenants in The King's African Rifles. Lionel brought them into my office. The two towered above him and I introduced them to the Governor in whom they met their match in height, but not in girth. One was Shaban Opolot from Acholi and the other was Idi Amin from the West Nile district. (You may remember that he handed over his platoon to Jimmy Fleming on Nkokonjeru hill in the course of the Bukedi riots.) They had each been recruited to the ranks and promoted in due course to sergeant and then to sergeant major. Amin has a reputation both as a rugby player and as a boxer; he is Uganda's heavyweight boxing champion. Neither had been sent for training to the Royal Military Academy at Sandhurst and their promotion seems to have been a last-minute attempt to increase the number of African officers. Only one or two younger and better educated Ugandans have been sent to Sandhurst. HE chatted to them, but they had rather little to say. Afterwards I went down with them to the garden where a photograph was taken with the Governor standing between these two giants.

As HE and I returned to our offices we walked up the stairs where the walls are lined with pictures of each of Uganda's governors, beginning with Sir Hesketh Bell in 1907. He had been promoted from commissioner, the rank in which he was appointed in 1905. As such he was the fourth successor to Sir Gerald Portal who in 1893 had been sent to Uganda to consider its future, consequent upon the British East Africa Company's fateful decision to withdraw.

Sir Hesketh Bell's photograph has special significance in that he built GH, albeit not the later office wing. On his arrival Sir Hesketh was "delighted with almost everything I find here. I cannot say much, for Government House. It is a very large bungalow of wood and iron, raised high on piles, and is as ugly and prosaic a building as one would not wish to see. I hope, before I leave Uganda, to have something much better than this. I have already cast my eye on a delightful eminence, at the back of the town, from which there is a wonderful view of the Lake and on which the Government House of the future ought, I think, to stand."[1] He next persuaded the Colonial Office to approve the sale of the dreaded bungalow for £3,500 to a South African businessman who wanted to turn it into a hotel. The site for the new GH was "only a bare, rounded knoll, covered with short grass, and is occupied by a rough mud hut serving as a signal station for the police. The soil appears to be excellent and, as everything grows here with marvellous rapidity, a beautiful garden can soon be created. There is a large amount of vacant ground at the back of the hill, which could provide considerable extensions of the grounds when needed. The house will command very lovely views over the golf course and foreshore."[2] The Baganda living along the lake shores at that time suffered severely from sleeping sickness which was spread by tsetse flies. I told you that Sir Hesketh drew up a scheme to resettle all the people further inland and cut down some of the forest. This had the effect of making the countryside around Entebbe even less tropical in appearance. In this environment Sir Hesketh thought that the new Government House should be "a really comfortable English house, such as one might find in the southern counties, rather than attempt to concoct some hybrid African or Indian construction which might prove an eyesore. The house is therefore of the big 'villa' type with very spacious verandas on the ground floor. The reception rooms are large and lofty and nearly every bedroom has its own entirely private little balcony commanding views over the lake that will make early breakfast a pure delight. Considering its size and general amenities, the cost, including furniture has been remarkably small. Even with the gardens and outbuildings, the total outlay will not much exceed £7,000."[3]

Over the years the original convoluted and corrugated-iron roof has been replaced with tiles and the Cohens added an upper floor above the kitchens for bedrooms for their children. I am not sure when the office wing was built, but on the stairs Sir Hesketh's photograph reminds us of the origins of this grand and lovely house. The main entrance, under the porte-cochère, leads past two magnificent elephant tusks, which must be some eight feet high, into a panelled hall. The walls of the grand staircase are decorated with paintings of Queen Victoria, King Edward VII and King George VI. We now wait to be told who will represent Her Majesty The Queen at independence. Many would like HM The Queen Mother to pay a further visit to Uganda. She was so popular when she came here in 1959. It is fairly certain that HRH Prince Philip will not come as he represented Her Majesty at Tanganyika's independence celebrations last December. On that occasion he flew from West Africa to Wau in the Sudan before coming to stay the night here. He was due to arrive for a late dinner, and as it is invariably the usual custom to dress for dinner every night in GH, the Governor was in a quandary. He was aware that the Duke might well have boarded the aircraft in safari kit and yet arrive at the airport in a dinner jacket; in that case HE did not want to wear an ordinary suit when he welcomed him. So a telegram was sent to the pilot asking about the Duke's likely dress. The reply came back from the pilot, "I shall be wearing trousers." Possibly those whom he had met at Wau did not! I did not ask Lady Coutts, who told me about this, how the Governor then solved this problem. She added that the Duke had sent a telegram to Buckingham Palace saying, "Wau was a wow."

The Duke was accompanied by his Private Secretary, Christopher Bonham Carter, who much enjoyed the dinner party at GH. When Lady Coutts met Bonham Carter again at Dar-es-Salaam she asked him how he had enjoyed the journey, meaning from Entebbe to Tanganyika. He, seemingly having forgotten his hostess of the night before, replied, "We stopped at Entebbe, which was quite convenient."

Lady Coutts told me about this lapse when she, the Governor and some of my friends came to dinner in my house. This was quite a test for my new cook Aramanzani, who used to work for Edward Cunningham. Edward has left Uganda to take a post-graduate degree at Harvard University. (Joseph had been keen to return to Ankole for some time.) Aramanzani is very capable but I managed, by agreement, to borrow one of the GH boys to wait at the table. This was a very agreeable evening. How fortunate I am that Peter Allen wrote "You will be required to come back."

Aramanzani and his wife outside my bungalow.

[1] Bell *Glimpses of a Governor's Life* 114

[2] Ibid 125

[3] Ibid 183

17: THE ADVANCE TO INDEPENDENCE

We now know that Their Royal Highnesses The Duke and Duchess of Kent will represent Her Majesty at our independence celebrations. These are being primarily organised by a branch of the Prime Minister's Office under the direction of my old friend the Minister without Portfolio, Balaki Kirya. He recently accompanied the PM when he came to see the Governor, but he was not included in the discussion. I offered him a seat in my office. He may well have been surprised to see me again and, although we had had that friendly talk on the veranda of my house at Budaka, the shock of this confrontation caused him to remove and read a book from my shelves as a means of avoiding conversation. The Uganda Government decided that its administrators could organise these celebrations itself, rather than appoint an ex-military specialist who has taken on this task in some countries. Obote and his ministers made an early decision to change the Democratic Party's design of Uganda's new flag. It will now feature a crested crane in a circle in the centre of black, red and yellow horizontal stripes. Wittingly or unwittingly, this perpetuates an element of the Governor's standard which too has a crested crane at its centre. Two officials have been appointed to be in charge of the independence celebrations and the Royal Tour. A start has been made on the planning of the many events during the ten-day period when TRH, as we more briefly refer to them, will be in Uganda. I am involved in all and everything which affects the Governor and I am beginning to work closely with Henry Kyemba, a new recruit to the Civil Service who has been posted by Peter Allen to the PM's Office as an assistant secretary in charge of protocol. Kyemba is a young history graduate from Makerere University, and was born in Busoga. He was educated at Busoga College, Mwiri. When we first met he told me that the PM, who comes from Lango, was one of the senior boys at the time but that they had not known each other at school. The headmaster, the Rev FG Coates, made a point of bringing many pupils from different districts together in the school, which thereby became a focus for national unity. Kyemba obviously has a lot to learn in a short time but he is very friendly and keen. In a sense we are both learning our tasks together.

At GH we plan to increase our own staff to cope with the many functions which will be held here. The Coutts' daughter, Jacqueline, will be staying here in October and will be Lady-in-Waiting to Lady Coutts. Lionel Botcherby will be appointed Comptroller to distinguish him from two temporary aides-de-camp. One will be James Apinyi, a young police officer, and another will be Roger Wheater who arrived in Uganda as a police officer and is now working in the National Parks, where he came to the notice of the Governor. It is customary for the host country to provide an equerry to Royal Visitors; 2/Lt Gus Karugaba, who is due to return from Sandhurst in September, will be appointed to this post We shall also be appointing Mr Dennis Burkitt, an internationally respected surgeon, as medical officer in attendance. People have also to be found to serve as press officer, security officer, baggage master and transport officer. You may think that all this is excessive but TRH will be travelling to every province.

Lady Coutts has proposed that some alterations should be made to the layout of the bedrooms in GH. The suite prepared for The Queen Mother in 1959 is currently used by the Coutts and the new plan will provide a suite for TRH comprising a bedroom and a dressing room, each with a bathroom, and a sitting room with new French windows opening onto a new balcony. Sir Hesketh Bell would have approved of this addition! So the builders came whilst Sir Walter and Lady Coutts were in London for the final constitutional conference. In their absence I authorised a minor change to my house; by reducing the size of my bedroom I have created a small verandah which also gives easier access to my spare room. I took it upon myself one weekend to remove part of a wall, much to the consternation of the Sikh foreman from the Ministry of Works! He did not realise that I had acquired some practical building knowledge after my parents' house had been 'doodlebugged' in the war. The Sikhs oversee much of the engineering and construction work for government and in commerce.

Before I tell you about the conference, you should know that 2/Lt Idi Amin has been in considerable trouble. Since my last letter there has been an outbreak of violence between the Karamajong and the Turkana on the Uganda/Kenya border. The police here and in Kenya could not contain this and the KAR were called upon to restore law and order. A platoon commanded by Idi Amin killed 'an unwarranted number' of Turkana. This was judged to be an act of brutality by the Attorney General of Kenya who recommended that Amin should be prosecuted for murder. The first I knew about this was the arrival at my house one Sunday afternoon of Lt Col Bill Cheyne, the dynamic CO of the 4th Battalion. He then had urgent discussions with the Governor, who foresaw that Uganda's relations with Kenya might be undermined unless some action was taken against Amin. Later the PM came to see the Governor. His concern arose from the unacceptable political difficulty which he would face in the event of Amin's prosecution and punishment. Many people might see Amin's action as a firm response to the Turkana who are persistent cross-border cattle raiders. Obote thought that it might be possible for Amin to be censured and made to pay a fine. In the end the PM decided that no action should be taken. The Kenya Government did not pursue the matter.

There was indeed plenty of trouble at the London conference which was held in Marlborough House. Outwardly the coalition of the Kabaka Yekka movement and the Uganda People's Congress indicated, for the first time in Uganda's history, that a generous spirit of national unity was possible. At first the Cabinet sought to limit the size of the delegations, but so many special interest groups campaigned for participation that a large number of government, opposition, kingdom and district representatives, together with some from the Asian community, eventually left for London in mid-June, accompanied by advisers and lawyers. The Baganda were determined to achieve as much autonomy as possible; the remainder of the delegates combined to frustrate that ambition. For some days it seemed that no progress could be possible in spite of the main talks, breaks for side talks and adjournments. There were repeated threats of boycotts as the arguments swayed from one side to another. The Governor and his officials strove to maintain the unity of the Obote government but there were times, according to Sir Walter, when it seemed that Uganda might disintegrate into four kingdoms and ten districts. Only the threat of a deadline produced progress: an agreement by 29th June or the postponement of independence in October.

There were particular difficulties with the Batoro, who sought the same degree of federalism as the Baganda. They were badly advised by Dingle Foot, their legal specialist, and the Governor told me that Obote had worked extremely hard to bring them to a more realistic attitude, holding long talks with them. When Sir Walter needed to contact Obote one evening he found that the PM was locked in discussions which ended at 3.00am on the next day, 15 hours after they had started. Later the PM said to the Governor, "You will have no more trouble with Toro." Obote felt confident that he could also do a deal with the Baganda. In the end it was decided that agreements with each of the kingdoms would be enshrined in the constitution. Thus, the entire period of British involvement with Uganda has been characterised from start to finish by the signing of agreements with different parts of the country.

An added level of difficulty arose from a dispute between Bunyoro and Buganda, the former having long claimed the return of the six 'Lost Counties'. The Munster Commission had recommended that this particularly thorny problem should be resolved by a referendum in two of the disputed counties in Buganda: Buyaga and Bugangazi. In these areas the 1959 census clearly showed that the Banyoro were then in a majority. It was also suggested that Bunyoro should choose one other county in which a referendum might also be held and that if the Banyoro were successful in any area, then that should be handed back to Bunyoro at independence. But this deep-seated issue which arose out of the Buganda Agreement of 1900 was not to be so easily solved. Lord Munster's proposal for a referendum was rejected and a Royal Commission under Lord Molson visited Uganda last January. This Commission's recommendation that two counties should be returned immediately to Bunyoro was held back from publication until after the April elections. It was not accepted by either party and the issue remained an open sore until the June conference. The Governor told me that whilst Obote was confident that he could satisfy the Batoro and the Baganda generally, he could see no way out of the 'Lost Counties' dispute. At the suggestion of the Deputy Governor, who remained here in Entebbe, the conference decided that the constitution should contain a clause guaranteeing the holding of a referendum in the 'Lost Counties' two years after independence. The Banyoro staged a walkout but could not resist the unanimity of the conference. So on 29th June the conference ended and the Governor and the Prime Minister concluded that sufficient agreement had been reached to enable all in Uganda to proceed to independence with reasonable optimism.

Since then, however, there have been a number of difficulties, perhaps partly engendered by the feeling of euphoria throughout the country as the day of Uhuru, the Swahili for 'freedom', draws near. With the advent of independence for Rwanda and Burundi, formerly Ruanda-Urundi, on 1st July there have been clashes between Hutu and Tutsi peoples in neighbouring Rwanda. There has also been some violence in Toro where the Baamba and Bakonjo tribesman have made separatist demands. You may remember that when I and two friends climbed the Ruwenzori we employed Bakonjo guides and porters. The idea that they could flourish independently is pure fantasy, but their demands arise from their separate identity and the distinctiveness of their homelands in the foothills of the mountains. They have nothing in common with the people and plains of Toro. There has also been more cattle raiding and lawlessness in Karamoja and talk of secession in Sebei, on the northern slopes of Mount Elgon.

It is very difficult for me to judge from here the true feelings of the people out in the districts. For some, the advent of independence will be seen as an opportunity for power and wealth. For others there may be a fear of domination and the likely loss of recourse to the impartial and fair judgements of district commissioners. I once saw a letter written by a complainant to his gombolola chief. In the fashion of our bureaucracy he had copied this to a number of others; in this order: The Saza Chief,

Sekibobo; O'wekitinisa the Enganzi of Ankole; Rubambansi the Omugabe of Ankole; His Excellency the Governor; God – and the District Commissioner!

Precedence is always important at GH. The seating plans for official dinners here require careful thought and knowledge. No one must be placed below the salt who should be above it, and vice versa. Dinner jackets are the rule every night, even when there are no guests, but there is always an informal atmosphere. I attended one dinner recently when the PM, some ministers and their wives and some officials, together with Charles Njonjo, a lawyer from Nairobi, and Martin Aliker, a dentist with an American wife, were present. They were all introduced to the Coutts' style of entertainment, which Njonjo and Aliker had encountered in Nairobi. In one game after dinner, a 'Quaker prayer meeting', everyone is made to kneel close together in a long straight line in the middle of the spacious ballroom. HE takes station at one end and says, "Let us pray." He then gives the person next to him a fairly hefty shove and the whole line of people end up on the floor. You may think that this is dreadfully simple but in our circumstances, when there is a real need for people to learn to know each other and relax, it seems to be very successful. As is also the game of hockey billiards played after dinner. In this the ball is propelled by hand up and down the table by two teams who have to run around the billiard table in time to repel the ball before it hits the cushion at their end. Quite often it leaves the table altogether!

You might deduce from the Quaker game that HE and Lady Coutts are irreligious. This is not so. Sir Walter is an Elder of the Presbyterian Church and worships regularly at their services in Kampala and also at St John's Church in Entebbe. Nor should you think that he loses any of his authority or dignity through his liking for party games. His sense of being Her Majesty's representative gives him an air of authority such that no one, even after a recent dinner party, is left in any doubt about his commitment to his duty or the respect which he expects. I always address him as 'Your Excellency' at our first meeting of the day and as 'Sir' thereafter. Both he and Lady Coutts, even at the busiest of times, always find time to speak to people, for example to Suleimani who waits upon events at the foot of the stairs to the offices.

Lady Coutts has numerous commitments to her work with various charities. There is a tradition in the administration that wives, whether up country or in Kampala or Entebbe, should be active in work amongst women, teaching them hygiene and care for their babies, or assisting the Red Cross and the Girl Guides. Lady Coutts' secretary, Pam Parker, will unfortunately return to England in August and I have suggested to Lady Coutts that Joanna Branchflower should be her new secretary. Basil, my colleague out at Budaka, married Joanna while on leave. Unhappily he was quite soon stricken with paralysis but is able to work at the Ministry of Health, although in a wheelchair for most of the time. Joanna's involvement here will mean that Basil can become involved with some of the life in GH, a distraction from his serious illness. They had met the Governor and Lady Coutts in London at a party during the conference.

I must conclude this letter. The country is vibrant, worried to some extent, excited and eager for the 8th October. There is so much work still to be done, not just in respect of independence. We are approaching the centenary of Speke's discovery of the source of the White Nile and I must begin to draft HE's speech for that occasion.

18: FREEDOM

I am now writing to you from an independent Uganda. The celebrations and the subsequent tour of the country by Their Royal Highnesses The Duke and Duchess of Kent were exhilarating and very successful. When TRH flew away from Entebbe to Tanganyika three days ago, we were all left feeling exhausted; but grateful for their dignity and charm which ensured a welcome throughout their extensive tour.

First, I must tell you that the celebrations of the centenary of Speke's discovery of the White Nile on 28th July 1862 were a successful curtain-raiser to these recent events. Speke's remarkable journey initiated British interest in Uganda and solved the age-old riddle of the source of the Nile. It is impossible for us now to appreciate fully the achievement of Speke as an explorer; the distances he walked and the privations he endured. I included his description of the Ripon Falls, known to the Baganda as 'the stones', in HE's speech. "Though beautiful, the scene was not exactly what I expected; . . . the roar of the waters, the thousands of passenger-fish, leaping at the falls with all their might, the Wasoga and Waganda fishermen coming out in boats and taking post on all the rocks with rod and hook, hippopotami and crocodiles lying sleepily on the water."[1] Most people think that Winston Churchill was the first to stand beside the Ripon Falls and have a vision of harnessing the whole river and letting "the Nile begin its long and beneficent journey to the sea by leaping through a turbine."[2] Yet, three years earlier, an embryonic Uganda Development Company (now known as The Uganda Company) issued a draft prospectus: "For the supply of power it would be possible to erect an electric generating station to be worked by water power from the Ripon Falls. A cheap supply of power and light would lead to the establishment of various other industries."[3] That is only ten years after the declaration of the Protectorate – however, it was clearly more than a little premature. The actual impetus for the construction of a dam arose at a breakfast meeting in 1946 between the Governor, Sir John Hall, and Dr Barton Worthington who drew up Uganda's first – and only – ten-year development plan. In 1954, only eight years later, The Queen opened the dam. Its construction in the heart of Africa, and across a river which flows at the average rate of 620 tons a second, attracted world-wide attention. The newly opened cement factory at Tororo was able to supply a third of the 50,000 tons of cement. Apart from the remainder of the cement, 32,000 tons of other materials had to be brought 800 miles by railway from Mombasa. The cost of this project was £7 million, mainly financed by the Protectorate Government.

I hope that you might agree that the economic development of Uganda, within the constraints of its geographical location, has been reasonably successful. Beginning with the early introduction of coffee and cotton and later of sugar and tea, the Protectorate Government has provided the infrastructure for further development by improving communications and power supplies. Much of this could not have been achieved without the commercial and technical skills of the Asians. It has encouraged private enterprise in mining, and the church missions have made a great contribution to education and also to health. I need hardly add that we have provided justice and maintained law and order, basic essentials for progress.

By contrast, political development has been fraught with difficulty. The various agreements made by our predecessors with the Kabaka and his fellow rulers have, with hindsight, hindered our attempts at unifying Uganda, though it would always have been an uphill struggle to unify so many disparate peoples, all with different languages, grouped together simply by the accidents of European colonial rivalries in the 19th century. The second constitutional conference succeeded largely because of the decision to embody revised agreements with each ruler in the constitution. This created much additional work after Sir Walter returned from London, with little more than three months left before independence. The Deputy Governor and the Attorney General were heavily involved in drafting these agreements. Those with Ankole and Bunyoro presented the least difficulties and HE asked me, knowing my affection for the Banyankole, to go with him to Mbarara where he signed the final Ankole Agreement with the Omugabe. We flew in the police air-wing's new two-engined Aztec. On the way the pilot, Chris Treen, demonstrated its ability to fly on a single engine while we were thousands of feet above Ankole's grassy plains. You may think that this was a needless risk with HE on board. Later the Governor himself flew the aircraft briefly until we were in sight of the airstrip, not far from the Omugabe's palace and the Kakyeka Sports Stadium. We were met by the Provincial and District Commissioners and were driven to the palace. The very short ceremony was followed by lunch; everyone was cheerful and optimistic for the future. As our plane took off and circled round I could see the PC's car driving away, the Union Jack flying from its bonnet. Looking down on the hills of Ankole, I felt quite tearful as with luck and a more sensible timetable for independence, I might have become DC Ankole myself one day; even acting PC of the Western Province. I cannot think of a more challenging job, added to which there would be the amazing view of the Ruwenzori from the PC's house at Fort Portal.

The final agreement with the Buganda Government was not so easily resolved. At the last moment the Baganda felt that the alliance between Kabaka Yekka and the Uganda People's Congress did not give them sufficient confidence for the future. In particular they pressed for control over the police within Buganda. Arguments over the constitution were only settled after yet another delegation went to London at the eleventh hour. Then the Governor and the Kabaka signed the final Buganda Agreement. The Toro Agreement was signed a bare two weeks before independence, and at one stage in the negotiations a lawyer from London had to walk from the Fort Portal airstrip to the DC's house after his car broke down. Quite a few of us thought that London lawyers deserved to have some African dust on their polished shoes! (Especially Phineas Quass, who acted for the Buganda Government in litigation which had no real hope of success. On one occasion, after he had won the first round in a legal tangle, his supporters hoisted him onto their shoulders, dropped him accidentally and broke his ankle. He lost the second round!)

I did not go with HE to the three other signing ceremonies but he asked me to go with him to present the insignia of the KBE to the Kabaka at the Twekobe Palace on 23rd August. This honour had been promulgated in *The London Gazette* on 1st January this year. You might ask why the Kabaka did not come to GH, where the Governor holds investitures twice a year. By now the emphasis was on informality; both the honour itself and our journey to his home were, perhaps, a reward for HH's final acquiescence in plans for a united Uganda. I first telephoned the Kabaka's Aide-de-Camp, George Malo, and was told that we should drive up to the Twekobe Palace, rather than to the old palace. I was surprised at this caveat for the latter was rarely used for official occasions; one exception was the informal drinks party to which I was invited after my return from Masaka. So I double-checked his advice. On arrival we were shown into a small room at the back of the Twekobe which had a view across the compound to the old palace and we waited for His Highness; long enough to think how some earlier British explorers and administrators had been received by Mutesa II's ancestors.

Stanley was told by Mutesa I's steward that the Kabaka "cannot see the face of his friend until he has eaten and is satisfied."[4] Speke was shown into a lot of dirty huts on the instruction of Mutesa I and told to wait for a day as "the king could not hold a levée whilst it is raining."[5] Lugard, at the court of Mwanga, was shown "a place to camp. It was a wet and dirty hollow, and I declined to accept it, nor yet another place shown me. Eventually I went on the top of a low gravelly knoll of waste land, and said I would camp there. It's name was Kampala."[6]

We were luckier than our predecessors! Eventually the Kabaka arrived saying, "I thought that you were coming to the old palace." He then ordered his staff to give us champagne cocktails, and strong ones at that. After a while Sir Walter congratulated HH and said how pleased he was to present him with the insignia of a KBE on behalf of Her Majesty. There was neither kneeling nor dubbing and the Kabaka mumbled a reply in the style of one who receives such awards quite often. This little ceremony over, we were driven back to Entebbe in the GH second-hand Rolls, slightly euphoric and knowing that His Highness only bought new ones – two at a time.

The final Queen's Birthday parade before independence at Entebbe.

There was a splendid final parade to mark The Queen's Birthday in June. This is normally held in Kampala but this year the Governor decided that it should be held on the Entebbe cricket ground, with Lake Victoria in the background. Major General Goodwin, General Officer Commanding East Africa was present and the 4th Battalion of The King's African Rifles, shortly to become The Uganda Rifles, demonstrated their skills in marching as well on grass as on the harder surfaces of Kololo airstrip, the usual place for the parade. We were all delighted to learn that Her Majesty appointed the Omukama of Toro and the Omugabe of Ankole to be Knights Batchelor on 2nd June (Sir Tito Winyi CBE, Omukama of Bunyoro, received his honours earlier, thus he was senior in these terms to his fellow kings in the Western Province).

Later that month the National Assembly voted to join the British Commonwealth and Milton Obote attended the Prime Ministers' Conference in London during September when Uganda's application was approved. But, ever since the second London conference, there had been no evident agreement on a Head of State. The Munster Commission suggested that the appointment of a Governor-General might give time for the consideration of a Ugandan as the new Head of State. The former Governor of Tanganyika, Sir Richard Turnbull, is now the Governor-General of Tanzania and his appointment was seen as a possible precedent. (I am glad that there is no intention to change the name Uganda – it has such an exciting and rounded resonance when pronounced slowly.) Obote is a close man and one driven more by political astuteness and skill than by a consistent political philosophy. So there was considerable uncertainty in the country, not least here at GH because Sir Walter and Lady Coutts needed to plan their own futures. The Governor could hardly ask Obote about his intention of appointing someone (who might be himself) as Head of State. I invited Frank Kalimuzo, now Permanent Secretary to the Prime Minister, more than once to drinks at my bungalow in the vain hope of eliciting news. I learnt no more when he asked me back to his house! So Sir Walter asked the Colonial Office if the Secretary of State could sound out Obote's intention and Duncan Sandys wrote to the Prime Minister on 3rd August. On 16th August Obote wrote both to the Secretary of State and to Sir Walter indicating that he and his Cabinet, and all the rulers, were agreed that Sir Walter should become the Governor-General. To Sir Walter he wrote:

> My Colleagues and I are highly appreciative of the able and dedicated manner in which you have assisted Uganda through her final stages to independent nationhood. The measurement of a job as has been yours here, is not in its length but rather in its character and as you remember I do believe very strongly in the principle behind that passage in the Speech from the Throne that "We are within sight of the top, but as with most mountain climbs, the final cliffs are the steepest and most baffling of all."[7]

The appointment is to be for one year with the possibility of an extension. Sir Walter and Lady Coutts then asked me to stay on as their Official Secretary and I readily agreed. (Governor-Generals do not have Private Secretaries for a reason which is not entirely clear.) It is just too soon to try to tell you how much I have been privileged to work with Sir Walter and Lady Coutts. They are greatly admired and respected by all who meet them.

A public announcement had to be delayed until the Constitution was enacted and Prime Minister Macmillan did not formally submit Sir Walter's name to The Queen until 13th September. On 19th September I wrote to the Colonial Office, having heard nothing from the Commonwealth Relations Office, to enquire when the Commission for the Governor-General would be received, and to obtain details of procedures and protocol arising out of the change from Governor to Governor-General. The Commission was signed by The Queen on 2nd October and arrived at Entebbe on 5th October, just in time for counter-signature by the Prime Minister and the announcement of the appointment on that day. This came far too late for the name of the new Governor-General to be included in the independence programmes and other publicity. In the end we sent Lionel Botcherby to GH Dar-es-Salaam to investigate their changed procedures and protocol.

Alongside all these last minute constitutional problems the Household was in overdrive. We had useful discussions here in June with TRH's staff when HE was in London for talks. As their Private Secretary, Lt Cmdr Richard Buckley, had not previously travelled overseas with TRH he was accompanied by Sir Phillip Hay, their Treasurer. In July and August there was still an enormous amount of work to be done. Even with our extra staff there were times when we thought that we would never be ready for our visitors. We had to attend to the logistics of all the journeys, find extra cars, plan the menus, issue invitations, draw up seating plans for dinner parties and luncheons, organise receptions for foreign dignitaries and the press corps and arrange a garden party for 3,000. We also had to approve the details of all the ceremonies in Kampala and up country in which TRH and Their Excellencies would be involved. Lady Coutts is now also addressed as Her Excellency, being the wife of a Governor-General. We now informally refer to them as TE. Pam Parker and her husband left Uganda for good in August and Lady Coutts appointed Joanna Branchflower as her secretary. Apart from the main independence ceremonies in Kampala and elsewhere, which were organised by the Prime Minister's Office, other people planned football and boxing matches, an international athletics meeting, a youth rally, a canoe regatta and an aerobatics display by Hawker jet fighters.

It would be too difficult to give you an account of all the celebrations. They were all joyful, exciting and peaceful. I only went to certain events as I tend to be the one to run the Office while the Comptroller and the aides-de-camp escort Sir Walter and Lady Coutts. The Household worked very well together and we followed Lady Coutts' advice, "We will laugh if anything goes wrong." Some things did; more of these later. I will mainly confine my description of the celebrations to those which I witnessed.

On Sunday 7th October TRH The Duke and Duchess of Kent arrived at Entebbe airport and as the aircraft drew up, a red carpet was laid down. Then nothing happened and the Governor, in full dress, was left wondering if he should climb the steps to open the door! At 11.00am, by the Captain's watch, the door was opened and The Duke inspected the Guard of Honour. HE introduced me to TRH on arrival at Government House and I, in turn, introduced them to our senior staff, leaving Nancy Vincent, our recently appointed housekeeper, to introduce our butler, Arthur, who comes from the Seychelles, and the two houseboys who had been assigned to them. That evening, after Evensong at St John's Church, there was a small dinner party which I attended. I told TRH that I was sorry that they would not be visiting Ankole because the visit to the Western Province is centred on Toro. On Monday 8th October TRH had a full programme in Kampala; a civic ceremony at the town hall and a visit to the Bulange, the Buganda Government's headquarters. There the Kabaka asked The Duke "to convey the people of this country's gratitude to Her Majesty The Queen and thereby to the British people for the guidance we have received and the wide friendship that has mantled the relationship between our peoples."[8] The Katikiro thanked "all the men and women from Britain who had given their best to place us where we are."[9] Then there was a buffet lunch at the Kabaka's palace. After a free afternoon there was a short reception for 150 members of the press corps in the GH gardens.

The Governor gave strict instructions that the corps should all leave promptly as he had arranged a small private ceremony at sunset. With TRH standing on the balcony of their sitting room, accompanied by Sir Phillip Hay, Richard Buckley and the Duchess' Lady-in-Waiting, Lady Moyra Hamilton, the Governor and Lady Coutts stood on the lawn as his standard was lowered for the last time. As KAR buglers played 'Sunset', the standard was slowly lowered by Sergeant Barnard. He had rehearsed this brief ceremony many times but the halyard caught in the pulley and, while he swore softly, there was an obstinate delay before it continued down. The standard was then folded by askaris and presented to HE by Sergeant Barnard; Sir Walter was too moved even to say 'Thank you'. It was a very emotional occasion as we all knew that the standard represented justice, good government, peace and progress over many years. I later said to HE, "Your standard did not want to come down."

In a broadcast on the eve of independence Prime Minister Obote said, "We are of Uganda and Uganda is ours. Let us recognise that and pay our tribute to these friends from inside and outside Uganda who have helped us on our way to independence. Let us remember the best we have received and now inherit from the British administrators. I also ask all to give the missionaries past and present a special praise for the light they brought and do still maintain."[10] By then the whole country was in a state of expectant excitement as crowds made their way to the Kololo Stadium in Kampala and to every district headquarters throughout the land. TRH were driven to Kampala and given a great reception at a splendid tattoo. The Duke was extremely complimentary about the standard of the KAR's drill. The band of the 4th Battalion was joined by the pipes and drums of The Scots Guards and The Gordon Highlanders. Acholi, Baganda and Asian dancers entertained us; helicopters hovered in display. As midnight approached, the KAR handed over their Colours to the new Uganda Rifles in the ceremony of Trooping the Colour. Then HE and the Prime Minister went down the steps of the stadium to stand by two high flagpoles. At midnight the Union Jack was lowered slowly in patient silence, before Uganda's flag was raised to tumultuous applause and wild cheering by a crowd of 50,000 people. Sir Walter saluted the Prime Minister and left him to receive the applause of the crowd, a lone figure in the large arena. There was then the finest display of fireworks ever seen in Uganda.

So ended 68 years of British rule; Uganda was now on its own in the world, but wisely staying within the Commonwealth. It is hard to explain my feelings at that moment. Everything seemed unreal; could we really have handed over all our power? I was certainly sad, yet the ceremony was, after all, no more nor less than the planned end of our protection. There was little time for much thought before TRH were driven off to more applause. Sir Walter and Lady Coutts followed, their car no longer flying the Governor's pennant on the bonnet; instead a larger Governor-General's pennant flew from the roof, above a silver crown set on a crimson shield. We had debated the protocol of HE flying his new standard before his swearing-in ceremony the following day. We concluded that there could be no vacancy in the position of Her Majesty's representative in Uganda, so the Governor-General's standard was also raised at GH at midnight. Unlike a governor's standard, and like the Royal Standard, it flies by day and night whenever the Governor-General is in residence. It has a crowned lion above The Queen's crown with Uganda written on a scroll underneath, all on a navy blue background. As we were leaving, the crowds began to stream away and there seemed to be an atmosphere of cheerful goodwill; maybe the fireworks had taken the edge off emotion. One or two of my Kampala friends and their wives walked back to their houses and heard jovial claims from some Ugandans, "Your wives belong to us now!" But they were only joking. The celebrations continued throughout the night. Next day we learned that there had been similarly successful and peaceful celebrations in all the up-country towns.

The next morning there was an independence ceremony at Kololo when the Governor-General was sworn in by the Chief Justice, and the Archbishops of Uganda and Rubaga conducted an ecumenical service, which included a Muslim prayer. The Duke of Kent then read a Message from Her Majesty The Queen before presenting the Constitutional Instruments to the Prime Minister. After the ceremony Sir Walter went to Parliament House for the swearing-in of the new Cabinet and was brought back to Entebbe by helicopter in time for the first official luncheon. The helicopter's rotor blades blew quantities of leaves into the dining room where the long table was set for 30 guests!

That evening I was invited to the Prime Minister's reception in Parliament House before an informal buffet supper at Makindye Lodge, the Governor-General's Kampala residence, where TRH and TE changed before we all went to the State Ball. I was delighted to find myself sitting next to The Duchess at supper, but lacked the courage to ask her to dance at the Ball. Just when I decided to approach her, she and The Duke left to return to GH!

Their Excellencies Sir Walter and Lady Coutts pause before leaving for the State Opening of Parliament.

The State Opening of Parliament and a State Drive through the streets of Kampala were the first engagements on the next day. In the afternoon we arranged a presentation of State Delegates to TRH in the pink drawing room. It was not all that easy to filter some 50 delegates, including Lord Carrington and Jomo Kenyatta, in the right order through the doors of the dining room at the right moment. Sir Walter as the DC Fort Hall had warned the Kenya Government about the rise of Mau Mau. Being a fluent Kikuyu speaker he was exceptionally close to the people and might have been attacked when dealing with an unruly crowd if he had not been able to talk to them directly and forcefully in their own tongue. Later he had opposed the release of Kenyatta prior to the resettlement of Mau Mau detainees. But there was no animosity as HE introduced Kenyatta to The Duke and Duchess.

Then there was a garden party and we arranged for a number of old or disabled people to have tea on the veranda. I was so pleased that my colleague from Budaka, Basil Branchflower, was one of them, although it is very distressing that he is now confined to a wheelchair. People were selected for presentation to TRH as they walked around the lawns and I included some at random, including the Omugabe of Ankole and his wife – that was a very pleasant duty. I also re-introduced Sue Phillips to The Duchess – they were at school together. Sue's husband John is an agricultural officer. When TRH withdrew the people left with great reluctance; the gardens overlooking the lake are so attractive and there was so much to talk about. The rulers' cars were drawn up on the drive and I escorted the Kabaka to his Rolls – at least he now knew that I would never again fly the Union Jack in his kingdom!

Later that day, Bruce Whittaker, the Director of the Department of Lands and Surveys, came to my office to present copies of the *Atlas of Uganda* to TRH and HE. This presentation should have been included in the programme but had been overlooked. The Duke of Kent gladly came to my office to receive his green leather-bound copy and congratulated Whittaker. The atlas with some 40 maps and many pages of information will be invaluable to schools. As a geographer you would find it extremely interesting and well designed. It was printed here in Entebbe.

On Thursday TRH began to tour the provinces; first they flew to Jinja with a compulsory visit to the Owen Falls Dam and then on to Tororo, Mbale and Gulu. As a change from visits and receptions they were able to stay at Paraa Lodge and view the Murchison Falls by launch before flying to Kasese for the visit to the Western Province. They spent Sunday 14th October in the Queen Elizabeth National Park and were taken privately by themselves in a launch along the Kazinga Channel. I only hope that they had some opportunity to see the Ruwenzori Mountains. Sir Walter asked me to go with him to Fort

Portal and we flew from Entebbe quite early in order to be there before TRH arrived by car from Mweya Lodge. We landed at Kasese almost in the shadow of the Ruwenzori and were driven along the foothills to Fort Portal. There we were met by the District Commissioner, Michael Purcell, and went to his house where the Governor-General changed into his full dress uniform.

At the Fort Portal Sports Ground a splendid curved wooden pavilion had been built; speeches were made by the Omukama and The Duke, according to subsequent press reports, 'in a jungle clearing'! After lunch at the Omukama's palace the Omukama persisted in his request that The Duke of Kent should lay the foundation stone of his new palace. Protocol decrees that 'Dukes do not lay foundation stones' and the situation was defused by the Prime Minister saying that he would do so, but torrential rain caused the plan to be abandoned. We then had to drive at speed back to Kasese and we boarded the Aztec for the return to Entebbe where we greeted TRH as they arrived ten minutes later in the Heron of the Queen's Flight.

That night I was invited to the State Dinner – prawn cocktail, poussin and passion fruit soufflé – at which the Prime Minister, the Kabaka, the Archbishop of Uganda, Air Chief Marshall Sir Charles Elworthy, Commander-in-Chief, Middle East and several members of the Cabinet were present; as were Bill Cheyne, now CO of The Uganda Rifles and Michael Macoun, Inspector General of Police. The success of the major ceremonies was largely due to their skills and the performance of the men whom they commanded. Two of my old Ankole friends were there; Basil Bataringaya, formerly of the Ankole Sports and Welfare Association, is now Leader of the Opposition. Grace Ibingira is the Minister of Justice. It was my first chance to congratulate them, though Basil would have been happier if the Democratic Party had held on to power. I reminded Grace of his jibe to me at his house in Kampala when he said that if I had stayed in England I "would be a nobody." I told them that I would soon be one again – he laughed. But what a change for Grace, from student to Minister of Justice in about five years. It was a splendid evening and The Duke had private conversations with Milton Obote and the Kabaka. We saw that everyone had a chance to talk to TRH individually. It had been quite a day – for them, as well as for us.

On their last full day The Duchess of Kent opened Mulago Hospital. It is one of our show pieces and has 870 beds; it is the largest hospital in central Africa and cost £2.3 million. At the same time The Duke flew to Jinja to see more of The Uganda Rifles. That night Sir Walter and Lady Coutts had a few friends to dinner which ended with 'games' – hockey billiards and a declaration by The Duke that it was "the best mess night that I have attended for a long time." TRH left early the next day. As I said, we were all exhausted, but buoyed up by HH the Aga Khan's verdict. He told TE that he had attended eight similar ceremonies – none had been as good as Uganda's independence which had been flawlessly organised.

HRH The Duchess of Kent says farewell to Roger Wheater, Gus Karugaba, James Apinyi, me, Jacqueline Coutts and Lionel Botcherby at Entebbe airport.

But he did not know about the cold water and the cockroach! I had told Lionel to make absolutely sure that TRH's rooms were in perfect order. On the first evening it was noticed that The Duke was going down the corridor to Lady Moyra Hamilton's bathroom and word was received that he had no hot water in his bathroom. A plumber was discreetly despatched into the roof – someone had turned off an immersion heater switch. Lady Coutts then remembered that when The Duke of Edinburgh had stayed at GH, on his way to and from the Tanzania independence celebrations, a message was received from his plane on his way back to Entebbe, "The Duke likes his bath water hot." Could it possibly have happened that GH had been in the habit of giving dukes cold baths? Had they thought that this was part of a Scot's way of life? (In case you have not realised it, Sir Walter, a son of the Manse, is proud of his heritage.)

Then the cockroach; it is impossible to ensure that GH is entirely free of these large insects. On retiring TRH were given a damp towel to place across the bottom of the door in their bedroom as the final line of defence. One day, on her way to her first engagement, The Duchess asked, "What was that long insect in the bathroom last night?" But then – this is Africa. Do you remember my telling you of the transparent guts of that lizard on the ceiling when first I arrived in Entebbe?

[1] Speke *Journal of the Discovery of the Source of the Nile* 466
[2] Churchill *My African Journey* 120
[3] Westlake *The Story of Owen Falls* 10
[4] Stanley *Through the Dark Continent* Vol I, 190
[5] Speke op cit 283
[6] Lugard *The Rise of our East African Empire* Vol I, 376
[7] Obote *Letter dated 16th August 1962* PRO CO 822/2990
[8] Mutesa II *Uganda Argus* 9th October 1962, 5
[9] Kintu Ibid 5
[10] Obote Ibid 1

19: THEIR EXCELLENCIES AT GOVERNMENT HOUSE

MOMBASA
12th October 1963

It is almost a year since I last wrote to you and just over eight years since I first arrived here at Mombasa. I left Uganda with Sir Walter and Lady Coutts three days ago on the first anniversary of independence. I cannot claim to have been busy in this last year; when I returned to GH from the airport, after saying goodbye to The Duke and Duchess of Kent, I found that my in-tray was empty.

Sir Walter soon settled to his new tasks as Governor-General, one of which, on behalf of Her Majesty The Queen, was to receive high commissioners and ambassadors who came to GH to present their Letters of Credence. We devised a brief ceremony for these occasions. Lionel, once again the only Aide-de-Camp, met them at the entrance and I escorted them to the pink drawing room and introduced them to HE who accepted their Letters and, after some conversation, Arthur served champagne. When they left I noticed that only the Russians insisted on having a Russian driver; everyone else relied on Ugandan drivers. Ours were absolutely excellent, particularly Aloni. The ceremony was repeated when an envoy left, bringing his Letters of Recall; although sometimes these were brought by his successor. I used to send all these documents to Buckingham Palace.

Aloni and Their Excellencies' Rolls Royce.

The British High Commissioner and his wife, Sir David and Lady Hunt, stayed at GH for some days prior to independence; together with their parrot which Lady Coutts would gladly have PNG'd! We were all distressed by the early attitude of some of Sir David's staff who all belong to the Commonwealth Relations Office. Andrew Stuart, who is acting Permanent Secretary at the Ministry of Information and Broadcasting, told me that some of his Ugandan colleagues, returning from a party at the British High Commission, said, "We don't understand those people." Apparently these nouveau diplomats sought to reassure them by saying, "Please understand, we are not like the people who have been oppressing you – we are your friends." Andrew was brought up in Uganda as his father was Bishop of Uganda from 1931 to 1952: he thus has many local friends, more so than most of us. This was not an isolated incident; the Commission's staff made many such remarks, reflecting a policy of apology for imagined sins.

In spite of their stay at GH, the Hunts also never entertained Sir Walter and Lady Coutts at their home in Kampala. Sir David, in response to a critical letter from Sir Walter, wrote, "I did not want to do anything which might have been misunderstood." This behaviour by Sir David and his staff also came to Obote's notice and he remarked to Sir Walter, during one of his regular meetings at GH, "The British do not seem to be sending us the same sort of people any more." He and most people in Uganda have, I think, valued the openness and directness of generations of district officers. Remember how Kesi Nganwa wept when Eric Weir, always a firm task master, left Ankole. The people here are not used to deviousness. Sir Walter, who appreciates that we had to hand over our power, maintains that the British have no need to surrender their influence. The High Commission could have built on our record instead of seeking to apologise for our achievements.

Apart from this sad turn of events, the year of the Governor-Generalship was of value to Obote and his ministers who appreciated Sir Walter's counsel; it was also a steadying influence on the country. Ugandans knew that Sir Walter had no power, but his presence was reassuring, especially to the remaining and still vital British staff running government services. Most thought that nothing could go terribly wrong while Their Excellencies remained at Government House.

As I mentioned in my last letter, as a wife of a Governor-General, Lady Coutts is also entitled to be addressed as Her Excellency. Also protocol decrees that men and women should bow and curtsey respectively to a Governor-General and to his wife. We did not insist on this but made the rule known; it was followed by some and not by others. All of this arises because a Governor-General is the direct personal representative of The Queen and is appointed by Her Majesty on the advice of the Prime Minister. A Governor, on the other hand, is responsible to the British Government, is Commander-in-Chief and also represents The Queen. As the Governor-General's Official Secretary, I – as well as his Household staff – were independent of the Government of Uganda, but paid by that Government – as was the Governor-General. (As Private Secretary to the Governor I had been part of the British colonial administration.)

It was my task to ensure that HE, with his reduced responsibilities, was nevertheless accorded all the dignity of his appointment. I maintained a close contact with Henry Kyemba and we agreed details of protocol for ceremonies when the Governor-General and the Prime Minister were both present. Normally the national anthem (Uganda has its own now) is played on the arrival of the Head of State on a formal occasion. Quite understandably, Milton Obote wished to be associated with Uganda's anthem, so we arranged for the British national anthem to be played on the arrival of the Governor-General.

On a lesser scale, just before President Nyerere of Tanzania came to stay at GH, I heard that the Austin Princess, which had been allocated to him, had been taken down to the public works department garage so that the royal crowns, fore and aft, could be removed. An official in the PM's Office, not Henry, told me that the President could not possibly travel in a car bearing the British Crown. I made it very clear that the President would be staying with a British Governor-General in a House full of EIIR monograms – on dining-room chairs, silver cutlery, glasses, towels, et al! So I went to the garage and supervised their reinstatement; no more was said and the President enjoyed his stay.

Other guests included Elspeth Huxley, the famous writer. She came to lunch and interviewed Sir Walter at "the enchanted white castle of Government House. Garden chairs on a sunny veranda overlooking velvet lawns, shady trees, waters of lapis lazuli blue; iced drinks and silent-footed, red-sashed menservants – it's all pure Noël Coward; in will drift the bikini'd leading lady: 'Remember Ischia, darling?' 'Dubrovnik, surely, sweet . . .' In this setting a hard-working, plain-living lowland Scot with Covenanter forebears eats his heart out in repugnant idleness. . . While everyone agrees that a Ugandan should replace him, no one can agree on whom that Ugandan should be."[1]

During the year there were many engagements, 'opening this and touring that'. Some combined business with pleasure and I was able to arrange a memorable visit to Ankole when Lady Coutt's mother and sister were visiting the country. Her mother, known as 'Mrs J', likes to paint at any opportunity and gave me a watercolour of the view from an escarpment to the south-east of Mbarara, stretching across the district to the Ruwenzori. They were

On safari in Ankole, 'Mrs J' is painting the view and Lady Coutts is photographing the painter.

typically not visible that evening, so I drew the outline from memory and she painted it in for me.

Sir Walter's brother, Ben Coutts, who farms in Scotland, also came to stay and I arranged a morning's visit for them to some farms in the Kampala area, with the aid of a Muganda agricultural officer. At the end we all went at Ben's suggestion to the Imperial Hotel for a beer. Never before had the Governor-General been seen drinking a pint in a pub! Ben was badly injured in the war at Tobruk, a bit of shrapnel 'blew his nose off' and at the time he was told to bathe his face in saline water. On his return home via South Africa, his ship was torpedoed near Ascension Island. As it went down he was most amused at the thought that he now had the whole of the Atlantic in which to bathe his wound. Happily, Sir Archibald MacIndoe repaired his nose in the course of 15 operations. Ben enjoyed the 'red carpet' of GH and the kindness of our staff.

On all our tours, including one by train from Kampala to Kasese, the Governor-General was always accorded a warm welcome, but by June this year he became anxious to know whether the term of his appointment would be extended beyond one year. Obote had assured the Secretary of State at independence that a decision on any extension "will not be an abrupt one and that it will be taken in good time and in consultation with your Office and Sir Walter himself."[2] Obote's idea of 'in good time' was subject to his making a difficult decision about Sir Walter's successor. There was clearly pressure for the appointment of an African and the Kabaka was generally thought to be the most likely candidate, but not one who would be welcomed by those in the north and west whose three kings were each thought by their own people to be worthy contenders.

Meanwhile, on the retirement of the Chief Justice, Sir Audley McKisack, the Prime Minister appointed a Nigerian in his place. His Honour Judge Udo Udoma arrived in Uganda while TE were on leave. In their absence the Chief Justice becomes acting Governor-General and I had to arrange for His Honour to be sworn in by His Honour Judge Dermot Sheridan, who had been acting Governor-General after Sir Audley had left Uganda. (Although badly crippled by polio, Dermot gave some splendid dinner parties at GH. At the end of these we 'poured' him into his car, as he chose to stay in his own house in Kampala where his faithful staff were so good at looking after him.) I enjoyed showing our new Nigerian acting Governor-General the sights of Kampala from the comfort of our Rolls Royce. When TE returned to GH our staff helped the new Chief Justice to settle into his residence in Kampala.

So the days went past and drinks with Frank Kalimuzo were no more productive of news than in the run-up to independence. Inevitably, in this

hiatus, the pace of life slowed in GH. There were more evenings without
guests than with guests, but dinner jackets remained the rule and, after Lionel
departed to a job in the tea industry in Kenya, I tended to spend more time in
GH than in my own house. In this way I learnt more of the Coutts' life in
Kenya. Wally was posted as a district officer to the Northern Frontier District
early in his career and, after their marriage, Bones became the first British
woman to take up residence in Wajir. She became used to tea made of saline
water and ten-day walking safaris, with camels to carry the luggage. They
lived in a 'beau geste' fort, a long, low, white building with few windows and
bats for company. On her first night there Bones had to help Wally kill 40
bats with their tennis rackets! After that they slept on the roof, except during
the rains when temporary shallow lakes appeared.

The community at Wajir was small but inventive as some of the rules of the
Wajir Yacht Club indicate :

1. The Club shall be styled the Royal Wajir Yacht
    Club.
2. The object of the Club shall be to encourage
    sailing before the wind, swinging the lead,
    profligacy on the high seas, and seeing the sun go
    down below the yard arm.
3. The Club shall consist of Ordinary Members,
    Extraordinary Members and Most Amazing
    Members. An Ordinary Member is deemed to
    have become an Extraordinary Member after
    three months in Wajir.
5. A Member who pays his Entrance Fee or Annual
    Subscription shall be deemed a Most Amazing
    Member.
7. Officers of His Majesty's Navy, Army and Air
    Force shall be considered "thirsty members"
    during their stay in Wajir.
8. The wives and lady friends ("sweeties") of
    members are welcomed to the Club at any time of
    the day or night at owner's risk.
11. Any article found in or near the Club must be
    returned to the owners. This does not include
    wives or sweeties of members.

One 'extraordinary member' was the district doctor. He tended to arrive
at the Coutts' residence at meal times because he had failed, yet again, to

Margaret and Penny on [.]
[.] final visit to Uganda.

order his food from Nairobi. Bones eventually advised him in strong terms to get his act together and he then told her to look out next day at breakfast time, as he had now found a new way of organising his meals. Looking from the roof soon after dawn, she saw him walking towards a camel, carrying two buckets and wearing a sarong and muslim hat. One bucket contained water and he used this to wash the camel's teats; into the other he milked the camel – until it kicked the bucket over and disappeared towards the horizon. Bones did not ask him in to breakfast; later, when she was pregnant, he refused to look after her – which was probably just as well! So she travelled to Nairobi with the Chief Secretary at the end of his visit to the Province and gave birth to Jacqueline. The doctor was posted to a less stressful appointment.

I paid a last visit to Kenya to see Margaret and John. Wally suggested that I drive his new Mercedes so that it will have some more miles on the clock when it arrives in the UK. They have a personal number plate, PPC 1. As Bones said, "We take our leave from our hosts as we drive away from their homes!" So Wally and Bones' time in Africa drew to an end with talk of their early days. The Prime Minister eventually informed Sir Walter that he intended to ask The Queen to appoint the Kabaka of Buganda as President of Uganda on the first anniversary of independence.

Meanwhile I became ill and chose to have an operation on a defective kidney in Mulago Hospital, rather than to leave prematurely; although I was told that a London surgeon would perform several of the required operations a month while Sir John Croot, formerly Minister of Health in the Protectorate Government, did two or three a year. I put my faith in Sir John and left for the hospital after a lunch which Bones had chosen – steak and kidney pie! The operation was a success, the kidney was saved and the nurses, both British and Ugandan, were extremely kind and efficient. The Coutts invited me to spend my last weeks in GH, having packed up my house, at Bones' insistence, before I went to hospital. Ten days later she and Wally came to collect me in the new Daimler. Wally sat in the front with Aloni – I could not have had a finer Aide-de-Camp! The limosine had been bought by the Government to replace the prematurely ageing Austin Princess. This had broken down during the independence celebrations – not something which occurred in HH the Kabaka's fleet of Rolls Royces.

Convalescence would have been difficult at GH as it would have been hard to keep out of my office, so a GH driver drove me in my car to spend some days with George Sacker and his new wife Penny at the stock farm outside Mbarara. He had met her while on the agricultural economics course at Oxford. I enjoyed being back in Ankole and they agreed to take on the care of Tosca, so I had to leave her there. It was a tearful parting; she had been such a good and faithful companion. While I was there I made arrangements to stay in Mombasa so that I could attend my sister Ann's wedding to Edward Bassett-Cross, before leaving for home by sea. Margaret was by now in England and I was again the only family representative – who else has given two sisters away in Africa? When I returned to Entebbe I went one evening to a small sundowner party given by Barbara Saben, formerly Mayor of Kampala, at her house on Makindye hill near the Governor-General's lodge. She and her husband had contributed greatly to the administration and commercial development of Kampala. She also founded the Uganda Club in Kampala, the first genuinely inter-racial club. She was awarded the CBE in the New Year's Honours and chose to attend the last Investiture at GH two months ago. As we looked out over Lake Victoria, she expressed her concern at the possibility that the Russians would seek to extend their cold-war influence into Africa.

At the kind suggestion of Wally and Bones I arranged a dinner party in GH for about 20 of my friends. We had the House to ourselves as TE were out at a farewell dinner in Kampala. Several of us had been together in Ankole so it was like the *Salad Days* of life in Mbarara where we used to dance to the tune of 'Memories are made of this'. This was the last formal dinner in the elegant dinning room where, to add to the nostalgia, we ate guinea fowl – fond memories of life out in the bush.

Wally playing a drum when he and Bones visited Suleimani's home on one of their last evenings in Uganda.

In our last week Suleimani asked TE to his nearby home where they met his large family and Wally played the drums amongst the banana trees. In return they were all invited back to GH and entertained us with songs and circus tricks. In one of these a large stone was placed on a man's stomach as he lay on the ground. The stone was then shattered with a sledge hammer! On our very last evening TE held a small dinner party for the staff. Lionel Botcherby came from Kenya and Roger Wheater also returned. And so our last morning arrived. On 9th October the head gardener lined up the 20 gardeners on the drive and we said goodbye to each of them. They had kept the lawns immaculately, with the use of their hand-mowers, in spite of the custom of the gentlemen, after dinner, walking on the lawns to 'see Africa'. On arrival at the airport we were astonished at the massive number of The Uganda Rifles and the Uganda Police drawn up as a Guard of Honour. It took some while for HE to inspect them all and he and Lady Coutts then had to say goodbye to 200 dignitaries drawn up in three lines. The Kabaka arrived late, but for once this was justified because he was in effect already President even though he was sworn in later that morning. The bands struck up 'Auld Lang Syne' as we said goodbye to all the Household staff along the way to an RAF Pembroke, which was waiting to fly us to Mombasa. I think we were all in tears by then; they had been such wonderful helpers, full of humour. (Except for one drunken cook armed excitedly with a knife whom Wally had disarmed in the kitchen three nights before!) The staff gave me a table lamp carved in the shape of a fish and at the very, very last moment Milton Obote gave Wally a large traditional drum. It was with some difficulty that the District Officer who became His Excellency the Governor-General of Uganda manoeuvred the drum, his sword and his plumed hat through the small doorway of the plane, turning to wave to his last 'District'.

[1] Huxley *Punch* 'Africana' Vol CCXLV No. 6408
[2] PRO CO 822/2990 16 August 1962

20: THIRTY-SIX YEARS LATER

POYNTINGTON
28 July 1999

It is a long time since we met and I was surprised to hear that you have recently found my letters from Uganda, but I see that I did suggest that you might keep the first. Your idea that I should now, thirty-six years later, write a commentary on them is quite a tall order; particularly your question, "Could the British have saved Uganda from 'Twenty years of tears', to quote *The Times* leader of 6 October 1982?" My letters evoke many memories; subsequent events in Uganda appear even more sad in comparison to those halcyon days, although it is now clear that Uganda is making very good progress under the leadership of President Museveni. He is a Munyankole and was at Mbarara High School when I was ADC III in Ankole District. I understand that he is interested in Uganda's history and so your question should perhaps be addressed to him and to Ugandan historians. However, now is a good moment for me to attempt an answer, 44 years to the day since I sailed away down the Thames in the *SS Kenya Castle*.

It so happens that Mavora and I have recently attended a Service of Commemoration and Thanksgiving at Westminster Abbey to mark the end of Her Majesty's Overseas Civil Service, the centenary of the Corona Club and the Golden Jubilee of Corona Worldwide. This was attended by Her Majesty The Queen and His Royal Highness The Duke of Edinburgh. At the Service I met several friends whom I had not seen for 36 years or so and we enjoyed a reception at St James's Palace, where the champagne flowed; at our expense – thinking of your taxes! Buckingham Palace, more mindful of our efforts and of history, referred in the Court Circular the following day to Her Majesty's attendance at a Service of Commemoration and Thanksgiving "for *the work of the Colonial* and Overseas Civil Services . . ."

More pertinent to your question, I then attended a conference on 'Administering Empire' at London University This was organised by the Institute of Commonwealth Studies and by the Corona Club. The Club was founded by Neville Chamberlain in 1900 as a means whereby Colonial Service officers, when on leave in London, could meet Colonial Office staff and their colleagues from other territories. Addressing the annual dinner in 1921, Winston Churchill said appreciatively, "Never has there been such a varied charge confided to so few." Corona Worldwide was established to support wives and children living in the colonial territories.

The objective of our conference was to make a thorough and honest academic assessment of the people who served and dismantled the Empire. This could hardly be achieved in just two days, for the Empire was such a wide-ranging field of endeavour; in 1937 the Service was responsible for over 60 million people in 2 million square miles of territory. (The Indian Civil Service, under the Viceroy, was responsible for a further 400 million or so people.) I was encouraged to hear from your friend, Dr Michael Twaddle, at the Institute that 'recent' history is now of considerable interest to students and researchers and that it may be included in the national curriculum. Fortunately, the left-wing and American campaign in the 1960s and 1970s has waned, ending the deliberate denigration of the Empire and attempts to inculcate a false sense of guilt. Michael told me that there are now calls for a fair appraisal of our record and a new fascination among the young, now denied the privileges which I and such a small number of colleagues enjoyed. It is intriguing that our aid workers and UN officials have been respectively described by Lord Hurd and Ferdinand Mount as today's 'district commissioners': our soldiers are now maintaining law and order in Kosovo, effectively a 'protectorate'. As Ferdinand Mount wrote in *The Sunday Times* on 13 June, "The old post-colonial guilt and resentment are melting away."

But, reverting to the Empire, the questions that are now being asked are 'How did our forebears do it? Why and how did it all begin? What were the consequences?' Today's students will find that:

> The history of the British Empire can be likened to a great tapestry. Its panels show an accumulation of hues and colours, of shapes and designs, of individuals and incidents; some sombre in tone, some vivid; there is struggle and success, achievement and disappointment, and sometimes failure. And throughout the broad extent of the canvas there runs a single continuous and unbroken thread. It is a thread that has marked the latter stages of empire as it runs towards the final panels. It is the thread that represents social and economic improvement, it is the thread of education and enlightenment, and it leads on to national consciousness and so to the conclusion of the work. [1]

My experiences can only be likened to a few small stitches in that 'great tapestry' but I will attempt to look back at British involvement in Uganda to see how it began and to attempt to determine why this was followed by those awful 'years of tears'. Could we have prepared the people of Uganda more thoroughly for independence; could we have influenced events after 1963 when Uganda became a republic within the Commonwealth? As one who was there for seven of our 68 years of the Protectorate Government, I have recorded some of my experiences for the Empire and Commonwealth Museum's oral history project. The Museum is appropriately sited at Bristol as Cabot sailed westwards from that port to America in 1497. Britain, on the edge of Europe, naturally looked overseas and, as a sea power, was able to lead the way in improving celestial navigation and the design of ships. Some see the Empire as an expression of capitalism: the Industrial Revolution certainly created a need for markets and for raw materials. America and Europe were enriched by the Atlantic slave trade; we were initially leaders of that trade but, "Britain through diplomatic action and naval force played the major part in the actual process of stamping out the slave trade. . . The leaders of the anti-slavery movement saw that abolition was not enough; they looked to the spread of the Christian way of life and to the development of legitimate trade to repair the damage done by slavery. Hence came the founding of a series of missionary societies at the end of the eighteenth and the beginning of the nineteenth centuries. From this flowed the great and expanding missionary effort in West Africa, as well as in other parts of Africa, an effort which has not only gained many millions of converts to Christianity, but has also provided the main means of developing education in the African countries and an important agency for the extension of medical services."[2]

So turning from this wider 'tapestry' to the 'Pearl of Africa' we, as geographers studying the human race in its environment, should begin with a map. The area now known as Uganda was first indicated on Ptolemy's map in about AD 150. This showed the source of the Nile near an area of lakes and some mountains, named by Ptolemy as the Mountains of the Moon. The origin of this name remains a mystery. I do not think that anyone knows precisely how Ptolemy acquired his remarkably accurate information. Maybe it came from Diogenes "a Greek trader, who, on returning from a voyage to India in about 50 AD is said to have landed at Rhaptum, somewhere on the East African coast from whence he reported that twenty-five days' journey inland brings one to the vicinity of a snowy mountain range from which the Nile derives its source and flows into two great lakes. It is not clear from this account whether or not Diogenes himself got to the lakes."[3] The source of Egypt's vital September floods remained unknown to Europeans for nearly 2,000 years. Exploration from the north proved near impossible and it was not until 1862 that Speke, starting from the east coast of Africa, surprised the world with proof of his earlier speculation. "The Nile is settled", he reported; but if he had not been so curious and determined, would the British have ever ruled Uganda?

Speke blazed the trail to the Kingdom of Buganda and was followed in subsequent years by Stanley, the Imperial British East African Company, Lugard and Portal – and not forgetting, as you have reminded me, the Khedive of Egypt's force despatched by your relative, Charles Gordon. All became immediately aware of the importance of Buganda, its existing system of government and its historic kabakaship. Sir Gerald Portal reported that the agreements made earlier by the Company were regarded locally as agreements made with the British Government. A less scrupulous administrator could have disregarded them and practised direct rule instead of indirect rule. To have done so would have certainly eased our attempts to unify Uganda; but the hallmarks of our administration under a succession of commissioners and governors were integrity and partnership.

Thus, from the earliest years, the Uganda Protectorate had at its core the large, wealthy and well-organised Kingdom of Buganda, jealous of its separate agreements with the British. These were given added significance in 1944 by the decision of Sir Charles Dundas to reduce intervention in Buganda's affairs. He replaced the provincial commissioner in Kampala with the first resident, who could do little more than give advice. This certainly made our subsequent efforts to unify the country more difficult.

Our administration followed a principle of financial self-sufficiency and held a belief, in Sir Andrew Cohen's phrase, that there was "indefinite time ahead." Financial self-sufficiency was based on the premise that "expanding services must be firmly based on growing local revenues, and that part of the process of growing toward political independence is to acquire the habit of financial self-sufficiency."[4] Clearly more financial help than a small share of the £1 million made available for all the colonies by the Colonial Development Act in 1929 would have quickened early progress.

In between the world wars, a time of minimal government activity, the pace of political progress was indeed slow. We should not be too critical as a certain level of literacy and education had to be reached; just think how much was achieved between the 1890s and 1939. "Look where you will, you will find that the British have ended wars, put a stop to savage customs, opened churches, schools and hospitals, built railways, roads and harbours, and developed the natural resources of the countries so as to mitigate the almost universal, desperate poverty. They have given freely in money and materials and in the services of a devoted band of Civil Servants; yet no tax is imposed upon any of the colonial peoples that is not spent by their own governments on projects for their own good."[5] You may think that this is a little 'rose-tinted', but it was a very neglected and wrongly rejected view in the intellectual climate of the last 30 years.

My old letters indicate the many political, economic and social advances made in Uganda after the Second World War. These were accelerated by Sir Andrew Cohen, a man of great energy, utopian vision – and impatience. He could not persuade the Kabaka to agree to his plans for a unitary government because of uncertainty about the relationship between Buganda and Uganda. As Kabaka Mutesa II recorded, "The Governor must be shown that in a contest of loyalty I owed an allegiance to my own people and not to the British Government. . . We had reached a curious position where Sir Andrew demanded that I should use all my power to help him implement a policy of which I disapproved as strongly as they did. The struggle was now personal, courtesy collapsing. Sir Andrew was talking in threats, and finally asserted: 'If you don't agree you'll have to go'. My reply was: 'If anyone has to go, it will certainly be you'."[6]

King Freddie was trapped between the traditions of Buganda and the advance of democracy. The fact that further progress in Uganda could only be achieved by his return from exile in 1955 showed the strength of his case; he remained unconvinced of the advantages of a constitutional monarchy. Babs Richards was right, we should have tried to widen his circle of advisers and friends. Almost inevitably, conflict arose only three and a half years after independence between the Kabaka as President and Prime Minister Obote. Who was at fault? Historians may conclude that neither were able to escape from the historical legacy that each had inherited.

The Kabaka's escape over the walls of the Lubiri and his pursuit by Obote's soldiers, led by Idi Amin, eventually ended in his lonely death in the East End of London in 1969. A harsh and sad outcome for one who was invariably, in my experience, dignified, friendly and appreciative of our contribution to Uganda generally. This brutal use by Obote of a greatly enlarged army was the seed of his own downfall and the 'years of tears'; Amin later used the army to stage a coup d'état in 1971. One of my colleagues, Peter McLean, who stayed on until 1965, was in charge of a development programme from which 25 per cent of the funds was devoted to defence. He told Obote that the 3rd and 4th Battalions of The Uganda Rifles were unnecessary and dangerous. Hubert Allen, visiting Uganda at the time of the coup, saw Amin's tanks halting outside the former Imperial Hotel, waiting for the traffic lights to turn from red to green! That was a piece of tragicomedy because Amin's regime, followed by Obote's harsh return to power in 1980, together led to the deaths of hundreds of thousands of Ugandans and the expulsion of the Asian community – the power-house of commerce. The world did virtually nothing. Only in 1977 did James Callaghan, the British Foreign Secretary, visit Uganda in order to secure the release of Denis Hills, who, in order to bring the wanton killing of Ugandans to the world's attention, had been describing Amin as a 'village tyrant' in a Kampala bar known to be full of government spies. Our rushed attempts to unify four kingdoms and ten districts into a modern, democratic and law-abiding state were set at nought. Should we really have tried to introduce British forms of local government? Were we right to expect that multi-party politics and the concept of government and opposition on the Westminster pattern would take root in so few years? I suggest that we really had no option other than to follow these tried and tested policies, as there was too little time to experiment with other systems. In any case the Ugandans wanted nothing less than the full panoply of our democratic system – the Speaker, the mace et al.

Historians may well judge that Iain Macleod acted irresponsibly in assuring his successor, Reginald Maudling, in September 1961 that "Uganda is all wrapped up" and in announcing, without consultation, that Uganda would be granted independence in October 1962, only seven months after the agreed date for self-government in March 1962. The continuing disquiet of the rulers and arguments with their political opponents in early 1962 was reflected in a Colonial Office minute dated 4th April from Leslie Monson to Howard Drake, which raised the possibility of extending the period of self-government:

> The difficulty about delay is that the last Secretary of State took the line that his decisions on the Wild Report and the Munster Commission Report, taken together, provided the basis for Uganda's "swift and sure advance to independence". Therefore, though events since October may suggest the advance has been too swift to be sure, we are stuck with the October date so long as all Uganda keep to the recipe agreed last October.
>
> On the other hand, if they depart from the plan agreed last October, it does give us an opportunity of saying, as the brief suggests, that the Constitution should be given a somewhat longer trial before full independence is introduced. . . We are not, in saying this, departing from the general line of the brief that the Kingdoms have now got to agree their status with others in Uganda.[7]

You will recall Macmillan's 'winds of change' speech in 1959. He was determined then and in the early 1960s to accelerate our departure from our colonies. Historians need to examine the reasons for his actions but I believe that they may have stemmed from the Suez debacle, and from left-wing pressure. "The United States and the Soviet Union were anxious to remove British and French colonial rule from Africa, not just for altruistic reasons but also to allow them to carve their spheres of influence. And in British society itself, a younger generation failed to be impressed by the lure of colonial service in far-flung parts of Africa."[8] It is also possible that Macmillan may have had fears that the Belgians' debacle in the Congo might be repeated elsewhere; yet, unlike us, they had made no preparations for independence and had ruled harshly. In fact there was no great build-up of nationalist pressure in Uganda. Many of its leaders were surprised and worried by the speed of our departure; we could have stayed longer if we had earlier laid down a reasoned timetable for political progress; perhaps on the lines of my minute to Tony Richards when I was one of his assistant residents in Kampala.

I discussed these matters with Sir Walter before he and Lady Coutts left Hampshire in 1978 to retire to Australia, where their daughter Jacqueline and son David had settled. He told me that Macleod took no notice of officials in Kenya, or in Uganda; they were not consulted or their views sought. Whitehall's attitude was one of 'full steam ahead and to hell with the consequences'.

Whatever Macmillan's reasons, there can be no doubt that Uganda would have benefited from a period of self-government lasting more than seven months. Even in a year or two, more Ugandans would have returned from professional training in Britain and elsewhere, including officer cadets from The Uganda Rifles at the Royal Military Academy, Sandhurst. The availability of more officers like Gus Karugaba would have left Idi Amin in the ranks and much less able to foment trouble. Macleod's timetable proved disastrous. Lord Chandos foresaw in 1955 that "There is no quicker way of putting the clock back than by putting it forward too quickly."[9] We had indeed foundered on the Charybdis of advocating, as some do, the "premature abdication of our responsibilities" – see my first letter.

Viewed from Government House the saddest part of our hand-over of power was the deliberate dissipation of our influence by the British High Commission through Sir David Hunt's policies of apology and inactivity; not wishing "to do anything which might have been misunderstood." He seemed determined to learn nothing from our knowledge of Uganda. This attitude effectively terminated British influence in Uganda. For example, if Sir David had sought to build on Sir Walter's relationship with Obote then the Prime Minister might have been persuaded to be more cautious in expanding the army. A key to Sir David's antipathy to the Governor-General, and by association to all my fellow administrators, is contained in a Colonial Office minute to Leslie Monson dated 5th July 1962: "As you also probably know there is a well hallowed Commonwealth Relations Office doctrine on this. They regard it as most objectionable in principle that the outgoing Governor should become the first Governor-General but in each particular case they have ended up by agreeing – Sir Maurice Dorman, Sierra Leone, Sir Richard Turnbull, Tanganyika, and Sir Kenneth Blackburne, Jamaica. We shall no doubt have the usual haggle but I doubt whether we need bring them into the picture until we know definitely whether Mr Obote intends to recommend Sir Walter for this post."[10]

The possibility that Prime Minister Obote might have been denied his choice of Wally Coutts as Governor-General for doctrinal reasons in Whitehall is appalling. The fact that four countries chose their last Governor to represent The Queen as their Head of State after independence is perhaps the strongest, if least known, evidence of the friendliness which marked our handover of power. Do you remember the tribute paid by Sir Abubakar Tafawa Balewa, Prime Minister of Nigeria? At independence he expressed gratitude "to the British officers whom we had known, first as masters and then as leaders and finally as partners but always as friends." This friendship continues in the Commonwealth which is a major force for stability in a troubled world, an association which has been joined by Mozambique and Namibia, neither of which have had an earlier British connection. Three other similar countries have been reported to be interested in becoming members. How many people are aware of this expansion of the Commonwealth?

These good relationships have much of their origins in the work of Colonial Service officers, as exemplified by Sir Walter. Sadly, he died in Australia on 4 November 1988 and Her Majesty The Queen was represented by the Earl of Elgin and Kincardine at his Memorial Service which was held at St Andrews on 30 November, his birthday and also St Andrew's Day. From his first appointment in Kenya in 1936, "He was always sympathetic, amiable, easy to approach. But he was also realistic, definite and decisive. And although his own abilities might have made him on occasions intolerant or impatient, this didn't happen because he never forgot that the true leader looks after his men and learns from their experience as well as his own. There is no question but that he made an enormous contribution in easing the difficult transition to independence in both Kenya and Uganda. He was indeed a personality of major importance and impact in the last years of the British Empire in East Africa." Sir Frank Loyd, who was representing the Secretary of State for Foreign and Commonwealth Affairs, concluded his address by saying, "Wally was a wonderful friend who never failed to keep in touch over the years. I think the picture of him that I like best is singing his favourite 'The Wee Cock Sparrer' at the Caledonian Dinner in Nyeri, forty years ago today. Wally was a big man in every sense, who set a rare example of integrity and humility in a life of great achievement." It was a rainy windswept night and afterwards Mavora, Joanna Branchflower and I were welcomed by Wally's family and treated to haggis and whisky.

I was greatly privileged to be Private Secretary to a man of such Christian humility, stature and humanity. When Mavora and I visited Bones in Australia last year, she greatly enjoyed, in spite of ill health, talking about life at Government House, where party games cemented relationships between the old and new 'Governors' of Uganda. Just three days ago I was told by Alison Coutts that Bones had died on Sunday 25 July. She was a good example to us all, led the way in demonstrating the commitment of so many 'colonial' wives to improving the lives of local women, and was a dedicated part of Governorship. She looked after all her staff and was always willing to do her duty, though prone to complain when yet another member of the British establishment found a reason to visit Uganda in January or February. Looking to the ceiling she would remark, "What we do for Great Britain!" Never reluctant to be blunt when something was wrong, she was to so many a very good friend. Now she and Wally have moved from Government House to God's House – "There are many rooms in my Father's house."[11]

President Museveni at State House and his people are carrying on the work of making Uganda a united nation, in accordance with the words on Uganda's coat of arms, 'For God and My Country'. Christianity, an enduring legacy which the British brought to Uganda, has sustained an ever-increasing number of Ugandans in the past difficult years. The churches flourish, Ugandan priests, and even a bishop – Bishop Sentamu – are missionaries in England. For our part the very least we can do in our materialistic society is to cancel Uganda's remaining debts.

Maybe these letters could help Ugandans understand a part of their history, for only a few are now left who have their own recollections of these formative years. We made mistakes; everyone needs to learn from the mistakes of history if they are to avoid repeating them. I hope that the letters show why and how we became involved in Uganda and what we tried to achieve before, in his final despatch as Governor, Sir Walter concluded by saying with Mark Antony, "Unarm, Eros; the long day's task is done."

For my part, I was fortunate to have had so many experiences in my early years, especially the privileged role of working alongside Sir Walter and Lady Coutts in the Private Office. On the one hand, my eight years in Uganda still overshadow my much longer subsequent work in the government here in this country, even though we are still a world power, a major world trading nation and partners in the unique and expanding Commonwealth. On the other hand, meeting Mavora in the 'corridors of power' and the fun of family life provide a new dimension, brought full circle by Emma's ascent of Mount Kilimanjaro, uncompleted business for me, and by Richard's crossing of the Atlantic, a latter-day Cabot!

For them and their contemporaries in Great Britain, I would add that Uganda is presently an island of progress in a disturbed continent and deserves our support. Its strategic position at the source of the Nile, its natural beauty, and the friendliness and humour of Ugandans make it ever 'the Pearl of Africa'; at the end of this journey 'up a beanstalk' we should all, as Churchill wrote, "Concentrate on Uganda."[12]

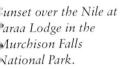

Sunset over the Nile at Paraa Lodge in the Murchison Falls National Park.

1 Bell *An Imperial Twilight* 234
2 Cohen *British Policy in Changing Africa* 7, 8
3 Langlands *Uganda Journal* Vol 26, No 1, 8
4 Cohen op cit 17
5 Churchill *Uganda, Corona Library* – Ingrams – *Foreword* vii
6 The Kabaka of Buganda *Desecration of my Kingdom* 120
7 PRO CO822 2205, 4th April 1962
8 Royle *Winds of Change* 150
9 Chandos *Political Evolution in African Territories* – *Optima* Vol 5 No 1, 5
10 PRO CO822 2990, 5th July 1962
11 *The Gospel according to St John* Ch 14 v 2
12 Churchill *My African Journey* 209

POSTSCRIPT

I have written this book in the form of an espistolary at the suggestion of John Symons, prompted perhaps by my letters to *The Times*. The Editor surprisingly published eight of these between 1982 and January this year. In that period, I campaigned against the false sense of colonial guilt inspired by the 'liberal left' and called for a balanced assessment of our record in Africa and elsewhere. On 7 January 1995 I wrote:

Sir, Jan Morris quotes George Santayana, the American philosopher, on those "sweet, just, boyish masters" who ruled the Empire in its decline. As one such – from 1955-1963 I served Her Majesty in Uganda – I greatly welcome Jan Morris' call to establish an Empire Museum. There is certainly no justness in the British peoples' alienation from their past by the false guilt propagated for so many years by those on the 'liberal left.'

In today's unstable world it is now very clear that we, in the course of our policy of leading so many countries to independence, gave them high standards of justice, peace and security, together with such economic development as was permitted by the constraints of geography. . .

The Owen Falls Dam at Jinja was opened by The Queen in 1954. Let us hope that Her Majesty may be invited to open a museum dedicated to the record of our imperial achievements and, yes, of our mistakes, at Bristol in or before the year 2000, perhaps including a model of that massive engineering achievement.

You can imagine my surprise when I read in *The Times* leader of 1 July 1997, "The years of post-colonial guilt and imperialism have, at last, given way to a more balanced, historical assessment." I could not resist a further letter to the Editor, tongue in cheek, to question whether my series of letters had brought about this sea-change in opinion. You will not be surprised to hear that it was not published!

Ugandans have a greater sense of humour. Once, in the Amin years, Roger Wheater was walking along the main street in Kampala at lunch time and saw a surveyor taking readings along the central reservation, which separated the carriageways. These were at different levels. Roger asked the surveyor why he was working so hard. Without raising his eye from his theodolite, the engineer said, "Heads will roll if this is not finished on time." He explained that President Idi Amin had visited Paris, admired the Champs-Elysées and ordered the construction of a single carriageway through the centre of Kampala so that he could take the salute as his tanks rolled past, four or five abreast. With his eye still trained on the theodolite, the surveyor said to Roger, "Sir, we in the Ministry of Works are only thankful that our President" – lifting his eyes to Heaven, he continued – "has not yet acquired a navy and visited Venice."

GLOSSARY

Askari	A soldier in The King's African Rifles or The Uganda Rifles; also a local government policeman/messenger.
Buganda	The Kingdom of Buganda.
Muganda	A person from Buganda.
Baganda	The people of Buganda.
Luganda	The language of the Baganda.
	Similarly, for example, a Munyankole, the Batoro, a Mukedi, the Lusoga language.
Bagyendanwa	The Royal Drums of Ankole.
Bahima	Pastoralists in Ankole of Nilo-Hamitic ethnic origin.
Bairu	Agriculturalists in Ankole of Bantu ethnic origin.
Banyankole	The people of Ankole.
Bulungi bwansi	Communal work for the good of the country.
Effendi	A warrant officer in the Uganda Army.
Enganzi	The Chief Minister of the Ankole Local Government.
Gombolola	A sub-division of a saza (see below) under the control of a gombolola chief.
Kabaka	The ruler/king of Buganda.
Kanzu	A long white gown worn by men.
Karamajong	The people of Karamoja district.
Katikiro	The Prime Minister of Buganda.
Lukiiko	A parliament/council of a kingdom or district or of a saza or gombolola. Also a meeting addressed by a DC or other official.
Matoke	Green bananas.
Muluka	Sub-division of a gombolola (see above) under the control of a muluka chief.
Nilotic	An ethnic group who came into Uganda from the north.
Omugabe	The ruler/king of Ankole.
Omukama	The rulers/kings of Bunyoro and Toro.
Rondavel	A round thatched hut or octagonal aluminium hut.
Runyankore	The language of the Banyankole.
Saza	A sub-division of a district under the control of a saza chief.
Shamba	A cultivated area usually around a homestead.

BIBLIOGRAPHY

* BELL, Sir Gawain: *An Imperial Twilight* (IB Tauris and Co Ltd, London, 1989)

BELL, Sir Hesketh: *Glimpses of a Governor's Life. From Diaries, Letters and Memoranda* (Sampson Low, London, 1946)

BERE, Rennie: *The Way to the Mountains of the Moon* (Arthur Barker, London, 1966)

* BRADLEY, Kenneth: *A Career in the Oversea Civil Service* (HMSO, London, 1955)

* CHANDOS, Lord: *Optima – A Quarterly Review* (Anglo American Corporation of South Africa Ltd, Johannesburg, 1955)

* CHURCHILL, Sir Winston: *My African Journey* (Hodder & Stoughton, London, 1908)

* COHEN, Sir Andrew: *British Policy in Changing Africa* (Routledge & Kegan Paul, London, 1959)

FORD, J: *Tsetse Fly in Ankole: A Hima Song* (Uganda Journal Vol 17 No2 1953)

LANGLANDS, BW: *Concepts of the Nile* (Uganda Journal Vol 26 No 1 1962)

LOW, Anthony: *British Public Opinion and the Uganda Question* (Uganda Journal Vol 18 No 2 1954)

* LUGARD, Capt Frederick: *The Rise of Our East African Empire* (Blackwood, Edinburgh & London 1893)

* MORRIS, Henry: *The Murder of Harry St George Galt* (Uganda Journal Vol 24 No 1 1960)

* MUTESA II, Sir Edward: *Desecration of my Kingdom* (Constable, London, 1967)

PORTAL, Sir Gerald: *The British Mission to Uganda in 1893* (Arnold, London, 1894)

* ROYLE, Trevor: *Winds of Change, The End of Empire in Africa* (John Murray, London, 1996)

SPEKE, John: *Journal of The Discovery of The Source of The Nile* (Blackwood, Edinburgh & London, 1863)

STANLEY, Henry: *Through the Dark Continent* Vols I and II (Sampson Law, London, 1878)   *In Darkest Africa* Vols I and II (Sampson Law, London, 1890)

THOMAS, HB: *More Early Treaties in Uganda* (Uganda Journal Vol 13 No 2 1949)

WESTLAKE, CR: *The Story of Owen Falls* (Uganda Electricity Board, Programme 26 April 1954)